TWO FOR JOY

TWO FOR JOY

The untold ways to enjoy
the countryside

ADAM HENSON

with Vernon Harwood

SPHERE

SPHERE

First published in Great Britain in 2022 by Sphere

3 5 7 9 10 8 6 4 2

Copyright © 2022 by Adam Henson
Original illustrations by Meghan Shepherd
Other images from Shutterstock and iStock

A CIP catalogue record for this book
is available from the British Library.

Hardback ISBN 978-1-4087-2736-2

Typeset in Palatino by M Rules
Printed and bound in Great Britain by Clays Ltd, Elcograf S.p.A

Papers used by Sphere are from well-managed forests and other
responsible sources.

MIX
Paper from
responsible sources
FSC

I'd like to dedicate this book to my wife Charlie. We thoroughly enjoy long walks in the countryside, and both have a love for the natural world. It provides a great source of pleasure through its visual beauty, the endless ability to learn and the opportunity for our senses to revel in every changing moment.

Contents

Introduction

On clear, crisp early mornings when the fields sparkle with frost and the little lanes around the farm are still empty, I love to lean against the gate and look out across the slumbering countryside. If I crane my neck enough, and concentrate hard, I'm able to hear the distant chimes of St Edward's Church clock; the faint sound floating through the air from Stow-on-the-Wold, four miles away as the crow flies. For almost five hundred years a church clock has marked time in the old market town, close to an ancient crossroads in the highest settlement on the blustery Cotswold hills, eight hundred feet above sea level. It's no wonder there's an old rhyme that goes: 'Stow-on-the-Wold, where the wind blows cold.' Take it from me, it's true! But the chill is more than compensated for by the view I enjoy every morning, across some of the most celebrated countryside in the world. It inspires me to think that the soft, undulating landscape all around has hardly changed since our Iron Age ancestors first farmed here.

This farm, these fields, those hills and hedgerows, the river valleys, the green meadows and the beech trees on the horizon have been the landscape of my life. But I'm as guilty as the next person of not always taking the time to truly notice just how beautiful and harmonious it all is. Life and work somehow seem to get in the way all too easily. I was delighted to see the sudden love for the countryside and the appreciation for nature that was expressed by millions of people during the coronavirus lockdowns. In terrible times our surroundings served as an unexpected antidote to the bad news all around, with people having more time to listen to birdsong and notice the tree blossom in their gardens. I wanted to write this book to help keep that joy alive now that our lives have sped up once more. I've always thought of myself as a lucky man to live and work in the great outdoors, but I can't pretend it hasn't also brought me some headaches! Most people probably know me as a TV presenter, but first and foremost I'm a farmer, and being a farmer is hard work, I can tell you. So, in many ways, taking time out to really research the things I see and hear around me and gather together the stories of the British Isles and its differing landscapes has given me

2

the perfect excuse to stop and appreciate the wonders of the countryside myself. Crikey, have I managed that! I feel very proud to call this group of islands in the North Atlantic my home, and I hope by the time you've finished this book, you'll feel the same.

The title for this book is borrowed from a well-known nursery rhyme about magpies:

One for sorrow,
Two for joy,
Three for a girl,
Four for a boy,
Five for silver,
Six for gold,
Seven for a secret,
Never to be told.

Why is two the number associated with joy? Just about everywhere, seeing two of anything is a joy; two swans swimming on a calm river, a doting mare with her new-born foal in a paddock, two lambs suckling a ewe with tails wagging in the air or two brown hares 'boxing' in the March sunshine. Although in this instance, I think the old rhyme is clear – it's the relief and happiness in discovering that it's not a lone magpie that's hopped into view! In Great Britain, a magpie on its own has been looked on as unlucky for centuries, and while I'm not a superstitious man, even

I salute a solitary magpie when I see one and will him on to find his 'wife'.

I never take the beauty of the landscape or the wonder of wildlife for granted. Hand-in-hand with appreciating the natural world around me is the reality that there is struggle and conflict in the pursuit of food, territory and a mate. The success of the food chain depends on there being life and death, light and shade, yin and yang. There's much more going on within a field-edge thicket or below the soil in a neatly tended garden than meets the eye, as I'm hoping to show you in this book. Magpies are the perfect example. There's the bold, striking appearance and the beautiful iridescent feathers which shine and shimmer in the light – in total contrast to their notorious behaviour for predating on chicks and small mammals. Mother Nature can seem like a cruel mistress but we shouldn't be shocked by it – we need the magpies just as much as we need the chicks they feed on. Once upon a time, farmers were happy to have them around because they helped to keep rodent populations on farms in check. I hope I can help you to appreciate this aspect of the countryside, along with the newborn lambs and dewy spring days.

I've lived almost all my life at Bemborough Farm where we grow arable crops and breed commercial sheep, with a large area devoted to a much-loved tourist attraction called the Cotswold Farm Park. In fact, one of my earliest memories is the day my father, Joe Henson, threw open the gates of the farm and invited the general public in to see his collection of British farm breeds. He had always been enchanted by the historic, slow-growing livestock of the British Isles, such as Gloucester cattle, Old Spots pigs and Norfolk Horn sheep which were becoming ever rarer in the post-war rush for intensive farming and the drive for highly productive quick-to-mature animals. So he thought the time had come for a rare breeds visitor attraction.

No one had done anything quite like it before and just about everybody thought it was a bad idea; the locals objected, his farming mates thought he was mad and he was even told that the Cotswolds wasn't the sort of place for tourists! It dawned on him that it was going to be an enormous gamble, putting the family business and his own reputation at risk. But with the help of his best friend and business partner, John Neave, and the unstinting support of my mum, he forged ahead with the idea and in the spring of 1971, the attraction was launched. It was the first farm park in the world and a blueprint for rural attractions everywhere – an early form of farm diversification. Almost immediately the sceptics were proved wrong with people thronging to meet the breeds and dis-cover their farming heritage, and more than half a century later my dad's great innovation continues to thrill, and to thrive. For all his incredible work, he received an MBE in 2011 for services to conservation. What a legacy!

Since I was in short trousers all I had ever wanted to do was follow in my father's footsteps and become a farmer. That happened in 1999 when I took over the farm tenancy from him, alongside my old college friend, Duncan Andrews. And working on TV must also be in the Henson genes because in the 1970s and '80s Dad was a familiar face on much-loved shows like *Animal Magic*. Typically he'd bring one of his rare breed calves, a lamb or perhaps a little pen of wriggling piglets to the studio to be fussed over by that legend of children's television, Johnny Morris.

One of the precious things Dad passed on to me was an understanding that agriculture is part of a much bigger picture; that farmland is just one landscape of many in the patchwork quilt of the British countryside, and while we spend our days tending crops and caring for farm livestock, there's a greater living environment all around us. Take conservation grazing for example. Rare and native breeds of cattle such as Belted Galloways and Dexters feed on overgrown scrub and woody vegetation in a way that helps wildflowers to thrive. The blooms entice pollinating bees and butterflies while the cattle dung attracts beetles and bugs, which in turn provide food for endangered farmland birds and bats. Livestock management like that is a win-win and my dad was doing it decades before anyone had heard the phrase 'environmental agriculture'. Farmers take enormous pride in being the guardians of the countryside – maintaining and preserving the sort of scenery that inspires writers, artists and millions of visitors every year. It comes at a cost of course. Agriculture can offer a marginal existence with low incomes and a tough life for many farmers and their families. In the chapters that follow, I'll reflect on these realities, as well as the things that make country life so worthwhile.

I've made lots of TV programmes about farming – *Lambing Live*, *Springtime on the Farm* and *Countryfile*, of course – but it's only on rare occasions that I have an opportunity to make films about other aspects of the countryside. So in this book I'm going to share my fascination for British mammals, wild birds, stunning landscapes and rural traditions. You don't need to visit dramatic landscapes like the Giant's Causeway in Antrim, Cheddar Gorge in Somerset or Malham Cove in West Yorkshire to appreciate all these things (although I can recommend all three). In every corner of the land the earthquakes, volcanic activity, glaciers, ice sheets and floods which forged the British Isles millions of years ago have left the deep valleys, craggy outcrops, steep bluffs and broad, lush vales that we know so well. Geologically we can claim to be one of the most diverse nations on earth and it's that rich, complex range of terrain from the Scillies to

Shetland which dictates what plants grow where, and which creatures thrive. But if geology has wrought the landscapes we love, it has also shaped our sense of place and identity. If you're proud of coming from, say, Yorkshire, Cheshire, Essex or Kent then it is nature you have to thank. Rivers and estuaries, hill ranges and mountain ridges, woodlands and forests are natural boundaries and in feudal times those borders became the basis for the counties that have existed for a thousand years.

Two for Joy is a celebration of the uniqueness of the British countryside and its fascinating past, but in addition it's a journey through the seasons. I've often thought how boring it must be to live in a country where the weather stays much the same for the entire year. Not so here. I remember hearing the famous 'birder' and former *Springwatch* presenter Bill Oddie on the radio, being asked about his favourite season. 'Well, I like spring,' he replied in a heartbeat, 'summer's not bad either, autumn I'm fond of, and I've always enjoyed winter!' He said it with tongue firmly in cheek but I had a feeling there was more than a grain of truth in his smart response. I know that I couldn't choose one season over another – they all have their particular magic: a carpet of bluebells in spring; the warm rain of a summer storm; autumn's first blackberry; starling murmurations in winter. And, of course, working on a farm means I'm wedded to the seasons – lambing, shearing, harvest, plough-ing, planting all have their place in the strict rotation of the year.

With the seasons leading us, and with joy as our aim, let the following pages be a trusted guide to the British countryside – the things we can see, hear and taste as well as places to go and activities to do throughout the year. Whether your interest is in cattle or conkers, corn-dollies or crab apples, there's a discovery waiting beyond the garden gate and over the fields. Perhaps your family has lived in the same village for generations or you've moved to the country in recent years. Maybe you love rural rambles and weekends away or you're relocating to escape the city and want to swap the sound of Bow Bells for cow bells! Whatever your connection to the countryside, I hope you will find plenty here to surprise, delight and enlighten. After all, the more we learn about the coun-tryside and its flora and fauna, and find happiness within it, the more we'll want to cherish and protect it.

Accompanying me on this journey and helping to get down on paper everything the countryside has to offer has been an old family friend, Vernon Harwood. He's been writing and broadcasting about farming and the countryside for decades, and he first came to Bemborough in 1991 to interview us about our beloved rare breeds. I've worked with Vernon on all sorts of projects over the years, including a radio documentary about Dad and his life's work, and I know we feel the same way about the living, working, wildlife-rich countryside. So come with us as we roam through rural Britain; exploring the heritage, explaining the mysteries and even exploding a few myths along the way. Don't forget your wellies . . .

Before we begin . . .

How to read this book

As the year is divided by the four seasons, so this
book is arranged in four parts, starting with spring.
If you read it from the beginning through to the
end I'll be delighted, of course, but this isn't a novel
or an autobiography, so if you want to dip in and
out as the relevant season rolls around, it will still
make sense.

A note on walking

In each part of this book, I've offered what I think is a
compelling subject for ramblers and walkers to enjoy,
to help them notice things about the countryside
they haven't spotted before which are relevant to the
season. If you're not a walker, or you're an armchair

adventurer, I hope you'll enjoy the information just as much.

We're fortunate to have public access across large parts of the British Isles with footpaths, bridleways and trails in every conceivable terrain from sandy bays to rocky moors and heathland. But with those rights come responsibilities, and wherever you roam keep the Countryside Code in mind. It includes reminders . . .

- Not to feed livestock, horses or wild animals
- To leave gates and property as you find them
- To stay on marked footpaths, even if they are muddy, to protect crops and wildlife
- And to always keep dogs on a lead or under close control

The entire Countryside Code with the latest updates is on the government website, which you can find here: www.gov.uk/countryside-code

Walkers and ramblers are welcome just about everywhere and have access to most of England, Wales, Scotland and Northern Ireland's best scenery and natural features. But there are restrictions on some routes and not all open land is free to roam, so it's important to check maps and signposts to avoid private property and the threat of trespass. I've included a guide to signposts at the back of this book on page 257.

Make sure you forage safely

There are many edible delights in hedgerows and woodland, provided free by nature, and I talk about some of them later. Bear in mind, however, that not everything is edible and some harmless-looking produce can, in fact, be poisonous. Before you eat anything, be absolutely certain you know what you've picked.

The Woodland Trust (www.woodlandtrust.org.uk) is an excellent organisation with expert knowledge of what berries, nuts, seeds, fungi and flowers are in season and what's safe to eat. Meanwhile detailed information about foraging and the law is available from Wild Food UK: www.wildfooduk.com

SPRING

March brings breezes loud and shrill,
stirs the dancing daffodil.

April brings the primrose sweet,
Scatters daisies at our feet.

May brings flocks of pretty lambs,
Skipping by their fleecy dams.

From 'The Months' by Sara Coleridge

Introduction

Birdsong, bumblebees and bursts of cherry blossom – the signs of spring are everywhere and only the most cold-hearted curmudgeon could fail to be cheered by warmer weather and the sights and sounds of Mother Nature as she shrugs off her winter cloak.

Everyone knows that the first day of spring is 20 March, the date when the hours of daylight and night-time are exactly the same length – the spring equinox. Unless you're a meteorologist, in which case spring starts on 1 March. Or you follow the Irish calendar, where the season begins in February. What about the old country saying 'spring has come when you can put a foot on three daisies'? And don't Morris dancers welcome spring as the sun comes up on the first of May? Well, just like the buttercups that carpet our fields and gardens, you can take your pick! It'll certainly give you plenty to think about on that first walk of the brand new season.

Whenever spring decides to arrive, it travels through the British Isles at walking speed. Starting on the south-west coast it rolls slowly north across the country towards the highlands and islands of Scotland at about two miles an hour. We know this because for years observers from the Woodland Trust and teams of ecological researchers have been recording the seasonal changes as they occur geographically. The signals include the first sightings of seven-spot ladybirds and orange-tipped butterflies, hawthorns flowering, English oak trees in leaf and the return of swallows from their winter grounds in Africa. The speed of spring means that it takes three weeks to cover the length of the British mainland from Land's End to John O'Groats.

For me, spring is when the buds are bursting from the branches with their fresh green sheen and when the ornamental cherry trees on our farm drive start to blossom. Before my mum passed away, we would have our photo taken under those very trees every year. Now the profusion of pink and white flowers always reminds me of her. They say smell evokes positive emotional memories and although it may sound a little strange, I also love the scent of the soft wool on a lamb's head when it's just a few hours old. I wonder if other farmers feel the same at lambing time? I hope I'm not alone!

Aside from that, spring means putting on my best suit and tie for a very special annual event. Every Easter the Malvern showground in Worcestershire hosts a one-day celebration of food and farming, called *CountryTastic*, with the aim of introducing under elevens to the idea of life on the land. By the end of the day I'll have seen the look of wonder and delight on the faces of thousands of children as they bottle feed lambs, stroke a donkey or cuddle a goat kid for the first time. There are also cookery workshops, gundog displays, willow weaving and big farm machinery on show, and the setting is pretty special too. The Three Counties showground sits near the plain of the River Severn with the stunning Malvern hills as a backdrop. I've been at every *CountryTastic* since it started in March 2008, and I always come away impressed and inspired by the youngsters' thirst for knowledge and their interest in farming and the countryside.

Once spring has sprung it never fails to put a smile on my face. It feels as if the whole world is waking up and there are signs of new birth and renewal all around. In fact so many changes take place when we eventually emerge from winter that it's impossible to include them all here. It's been a difficult job choosing the ones which mean the most to me, but I hope my selection helps you appreciate spring more than ever.

1

The Birds and the Bees

One of the most joyful things about spring is the return of the dawn chorus – the unique sound of early morning birdsong which seems for all the world like Mother Nature's alarm clock. Waking up an hour before daybreak on a fine spring day, wrapping up warm and sitting outside for a personal performance of a musical masterpiece is one of the best ways to slow down and appreciate the countryside.

The dawn chorus is essentially the avian equivalent of speed dating, and it takes place from March onwards when the world warms up and the days get longer – meaning there's more food available. Singing is an energetic business, so the birds need to be well-fed to do it. The better fed they are, the stronger, sweeter and more spectacular the song they produce – a way for the males to prove to the females that they're a healthy mate. The dawn chorus is also a territorial warning: the birds are sending a message to their rivals that they have arrived and are prepared to defend their little domain.

But why do they do it at dawn? Well, when the light is dim, even if you're making a song and dance, it's hard for predators to spot you. In addition, at that time of day birds can't do much else – just as we'd struggle to find anything good for breakfast in a dark kitchen, so birds can't find their meal until the sun is up.

The dawn chorus is loudest in May and June when migrating species join the ranks of birds like robins, which are here all year round. This means that if you want to single out a robin from the cacophony of other birdsong, the gentler dawn chorus in March is a good time to try. The robin has a very varied, twittery song, made up of lots of different notes and whistles, each verse lasting for a few seconds apiece. Given how confident robins are, you're bound to have one land near you and chirp away at some point; try to memorise it and then the next time you hear the dawn chorus, see if you can pinpoint it in the wall of sound. Being able to tune into different birdsong is a satisfying skill.

My favourite songster is the blackbird. These aptly named black birds have bright orange-yellow beaks and rings around their eyes, although confusingly females have brown feathers, often with streaks and spots on their breast. Blackbirds bookend the day: they're the first birds to rise before dawn and often the last to roost after dark. Listen out for a short burst (no more than a second or two) of fluty verse often followed by a sequence of squeaks. There's plenty of country lore surrounding blackbirds too: an old superstition states that if a blackbird makes a nest on your roof then you're in for some very good luck, and even something as routine as seeing two together can mean good news is on the way.

Turn the page for a few more birds to listen out for ...

Song thrush

Song	Notes of interest
Similar to the song of the blackbird but much less musical – it repeats the same five notes continuously.	If you see pieces of broken shell around a flat stone, you've found the thrush's anvil – the very fitting name given to nature's version of the blacksmith's trademark tool. Song thrushes feed on snails and to get to their lunch they smash the snail shell violently against a rock or stone with a seasoned flick of the head.

Wren

Song	Notes of interest
It's loud, proud and can sing hundreds of notes every minute, some high-pitched ones followed by bursts of soft trills.	While it isn't quite the smallest bird – that honour goes to the goldcrest and its much rarer cousin, the firecrest – the wren is certainly a tiny bird and used to be featured on the smallest British coin, the pre-decimal farthing. I've heard them called 'the mice of the bird world' because if you get a brief glimpse of something scurrying around at the bottom of a hedge, it's much more likely to be a wren than a rodent.

Great tit

Song	Notes of interest
Listen out for a dodgy wheelbarrow with a squeak at the front! The two-syllable song of the great tit is made up of a strong high note followed immediately by a gentler low note which sounds like *teacher-teacher-teacher*.	They're among the most colourful of all the garden visitors, with green and yellow feathers, a glossy black head and white cheeks.

Chiffchaff

Song	Notes of interest
It sings its name! Listen out for *chiff-chaff chiff-chaff*.	This small green warbler is the first of the summer visitors, having spent the winter in southern France or the Mediterranean. Chiffchaffs eat caterpillars and spiders but their party trick is to fly out from a tree and snap an insect in flight.

Woodpigeon

Song	Notes of interest
The loud husky cooing of woodpigeons is the brash alternative to the soft call of the feral pigeons we encounter in city centres. There are five coos in a quick-slow-slow-quick-quick rhythm and it's easy to imagine the woodpigeon imitating the phrase *My toe bleeds, Betty*. Then for a finale, it always ends with a single short coo.	Britain's largest and most common pigeon. It's no longer found exclusively in woodland and forests but has expanded its habitat to parks, gardens, farmland and even urban sites all over the country. There are around five and a half million breeding pairs in the UK.

Nightingale

Song	Notes of interest
Despite what people say, it doesn't just sing at night. It can be heard at any time with its crisp fluted notes. It's a mesmerising song full of rippling whistles, tweets, trills and guttural chugs with a range of notes that's unrivalled in the bird world. Impossible to compare with any sound in nature, it's thought the nightingale's repertoire includes a thousand syllables and once heard, it's never forgotten.	It's a fussy performer, singing from the centre of bushes but only ones surrounded by open ground, so to hear one is very special. Various predators prey on nightingales given the nests are built low down in the scrub, so they are easy pickings for a hungry stoat or weasel; sometimes even squirrels will take an egg. Sparrowhawks will also take their chance and it's thought tawny owls take advantage of being night predators to help themselves too.

Song	Notes of interest
This is the noisy, interrupting motor mouth of the countryside. The loud chattering *chak-chak-chak* will have other birds scattering but the magpie's vocabulary also includes short harsh *ch-tak* calls and high *ch-ulk* sounds. If you're very lucky you might even hear one mimicking other birds' song.	Nothing else in the countryside quite compares with the bold, insistent and unmistakable magpie. The long-tailed scavenger with the black-and-white plumage is a member of the crow family and lives in thorny shrub and high up in tall trees. On average their life expectancy is about three years but the oldest magpie on record was a remarkable twenty-one years old.

For me though, there's only one bird that symbolises spring and it's the cuckoo. As the old country rhyme goes:

The cuckoo comes in April,
Sings his song in May.
In the middle of June
He changes his tune,
And in July he flies away.

Cuck-oo, cuck-oo was such a familiar sound when I was young, and being a country boy I looked forward to the cuckoo heralding the onset of spring. Though I hear them less often these days, it's still worth listening out for one around the end of March and in early April, because it's an incredibly exciting moment that will make you feel certain spring has arrived.

Their distinctive call is matched by their unusual appearance; imagine a cross between a dove and a sparrowhawk. Cuckoos are sleek with long tails and pointed wings which droop when they perch. They have blue-grey feathers on their heads, backs and chests but a black-and-white striped pattern, known as barring, on the underside. Look for the thin yellow ring around the eyes and their yellow feet and you can be sure it's a cuckoo. Being a traditional harbinger of spring begs the question, where do cuckoos spend the winter? The answer is central Africa and amazingly their migration route to the UK in spring is different from the journey they take back across Europe a few months later. Mystery still surrounds the story of cuckoo migration but scientists believe they switch routes to take advantage of favourable winds or to avoid bad weather. It's satnav as standard courtesy of Mother Nature, and I only wish the system in my car was half as good!

Their reputation as a much-loved seasonal visitor glosses over the fact that cuckoos are cunning cheats and brood parasites. As the phrase 'cuckoo in the nest' implies, instead of building a nest in the mating season, the female finds another bird's nest and when the host is away she removes one of its eggs before laying her own in its place. After about twelve days, when the cuckoo chick hatches, it pushes the other eggs or chicks out of the nest and then mimics the call of a whole brood so that it can steal all the food brought back by the hoodwinked host bird! As terrible as the cuckoos' behaviour in the nest is, I can't help but be impressed by their unbelievable survival instincts and navigation skills. When summer comes around and the adults begin their long migration back to Africa they leave their fledglings here, continuing to be fed by their hapless hosts and never having contact with their parents. Weeks or even months later, when they've grown their flight feathers, the juvenile cuckoos make their own way south to Africa for the first time, without needing to learn the way from experienced adults. It really is a marvel of nature.

Whether it's a cuckoo, the delightful call of a blackbird or the familiar coo of a friendly woodpigeon, listening to springtime birdsong is a calming, reassuring thing to do. Taking a few minutes to watch birds fly and flit about your garden or a local park is another simple and cost-free way to reconnect with nature; a pleasant distraction we're beginning to realise is vitally important for our well-being.

Putting food out for the birds is something that millions of people do, but it's easy to go one step further than just scattering seeds and kitchen scraps on the grass. Think about planting fruit and berry trees or bushes in the garden to encourage and feed our feathered friends. Holly, hawthorn, sunflowers, blackberry and elderberry are all good for starters and even wild roses, teasel, yew and ivy will bring them flocking in. It's not all about food though; just like us, birds need plenty of clean water to survive. They don't just drink it – they need to bathe in water too to keep their feathers in tip-top condition. If you haven't got a bird-bath, any shallow container with sloping sides will do. In the winter you can stop it icing over by putting a ping-pong ball in the water; it will bob around and keep the water moving when the temperature plummets. The more bird-friendly your garden is, the bigger the reward will be in the diversity of species and sheer numbers which visit you through the year.

Birds eat all sorts of food but a big source of protein for them is insects. Mating time for most birds is spring because that's when their food supply becomes bountiful – so it follows that spring is a great time for insects too. Bees, bugs and beetles might not be an obvious source of joy and there's definitely a limit to how many I'll put up with inside the house! But they are essential to the ecosystems and health of the countryside, and I think spotting insects and understanding what they're doing can be endlessly fascinating. Even the ones we dislike the most have hidden talents to appreciate.

When it comes to getting a bad rap, the bluebottle has to be at the top of almost everyone's list of 'filthy flies' and the Latin name – *calliphora vomitoria* – gives us a clue why. Yup, they have to throw up on their food; the enzymes in their saliva turn the food to liquid so they can drink it up. Bluebottles are a species of blowfly and their maggots can infest livestock, so they're a major hazard for sheep farmers like me. Nevertheless, these big shiny metallic-blue flies with their loud buzzing noise do play an important part in the cycle of life. Believe it or not, adult bluebottles feed on nectar and can help pollinate certain types of strong-smelling flowers. In fact, some plant breeders have used them instead of bees to pollinate carrots. They're also incredibly useful in forensics. Female bluebottles lay their eggs on dead animals and humans, and by examining the size of the maggots and pupae, experts can work out when the flies arrived and then pinpoint the time of death. Think of it as a sort of insect version of *CSI*.

If bluebottles are unpopular, wasps are our ultimate nemesis. Like everyone, I've had my fair share of disrupted picnics thanks to the arrival of a greedy wasp or two, and I'm more nervous than most as I'm allergic to stings and swell up unless I can get an antihistamine pill down sharpish. But like pretty much everything in nature, these notoriously insistent insects have their benefits. Like blowflies they're useful pollinators as they fly from plant to plant in search of sweet, sugary nectar. They're the gardener's friend in other ways too thanks to their voracious appetite for invertebrates; without them we'd be overrun by spiders, caterpillars and greenfly. They'll even consume other wasps! But the adults don't eat their prey themselves – they're carb lovers that only feast on sugars. Instead, they feed their victims to their young.

Spring is the crucial season for wasps and the start of their life cycle, the time when fertile queens begin looking for suitable places to build a nest and start a new colony. A queen will lay up to three hundred eggs a day and the young develop from the eggs into larvae, then pupae through to fully formed 'worker' wasps while still inside the nest. The wasps' ongoing survival hinges on the behaviour of the queen at the end of summer, when she lays eggs which become new queens and productive males. The new queens are fertilised by the males before finding a place to hibernate. Wasps are starved of food in winter which kills off the nest and colony while the cold weather wipes out many of the hibernating queens. The few that do survive in underground burrows, old log piles or inside lofts and garages will reappear the following spring to start the circle of life again.

So what other flying, creeping and crawling crea- tures have a surprising secret life?

Giant house spider

Life cycle	Predator and prey	Appearance	Did you know . . .
One of the 650 species of spider in the UK. The spiderlings hatch from the eggs in spring and are active all year round. Like most spiders, they come into homes in autumn when the males start roaming, looking to mate with females that may have spun a web indoors.	Giant house spiders spin sheet-like webs in corners to trap small insects, beetles, flies, moths and even crickets. In turn, they provide a tasty meal for birds such as blackbirds, crows and pigeons.	Despite its name this brown, long-legged arachnid with its hairy body isn't the UK's biggest spider (that honour goes to the cardinal spider) but it is the fastest.	Giant house spiders can survive for months without food or water.

Harlequin ladybird

Life cycle	Predator and prey	Appearance	Did you know . . .
Most female ladybirds lay up to 100 eggs in late spring, but harlequins breed all spring and summer so can produce two or more generations every year.	Their diet includes aphids, butterfly and moth larvae and other ladybirds. They will also feed on the juice of orchard fruits and grapes. Their enemies in the garden are spiders, large beetles, frogs and wasps.	Originally from Asia, they have become one of the most common ladybirds in the country. The variety of patterns on their backs is enormous with up to nineteen black spots on a red or orange background.	The first harlequins in Britain were recorded in 2003 and arrived here unintentionally from Europe; blown across the English Channel on strong winds, as well as transported with imported food and in holiday-makers' luggage.

Silver Y moth

Life cycle	Predator and prey	Appearance	Did you know . . .
Our most common migrant moth, arriving here in spring from the Mediterranean and Black Sea regions. They breed in the UK producing up to three generations a year.	The caterpillars feed on low-growing plants like stinging nettles, cabbage and clover while the adults will fly around buddleia and lavender in search of nectar.	These grey/brown moths are easy to identify from the metallic silver 'Y' on each forewing. The hind wings are lighter in colour.	Most moth species – but not all – are attracted to light, although experts are still unsure exactly why (a source of navigation is the most common theory; electric lamps and lanterns acting as artificial 'moons' which disorientate moths). Football's Euro 2016 final in Paris was interrupted by an invasion of silver Ys covering the pitch and the stands after the floodlights were left on overnight.

Stag beetle

Life cycle	Predator and prey	Appearance	Did you know . . .
A magnificent-looking creature in maturity, the life of a stag beetle is spent underground as a larva, or grub, apart from a few weeks in summer when it emerges to find a mate. Their lifespan can be anything up to seven years.	The larvae feed on rotting wood while adults have to rely on their fat reserves, sap and decaying fruit because they can't eat solids. Kestrels, crows, foxes and badgers will prey on stag beetles.	The jaws of the male look exactly like the antlers of a stag in miniature. The head and body section of both males and females is shiny black and their large wing cases are a deep chestnut brown colour.	The fearsome jaws of the male might look terrifying but they're surprisingly weak and are used to show off to the females and frighten rivals. Despite appearances they won't bite you.

Painted lady butterfly

Life cycle	Predator and prey	Appearance	Did you know . . .
An impressive long-distance traveller which arrives here in April, May and June from north Africa, the Middle East and central Asia. The females lay up to 500 eggs and after emerging as adults their lifespan is less than twenty-four days.	The caterpillars thrive on thistles and the adults will feed on nectar from a wide range of weeds and flowers. Their predators include birds, rats, toads and snakes.	Look for orange wings with black markings and white and black spots. The hind wings have very obvious rows of black spots.	Experts talk of 'painted lady summers' when as many as 11 million of these beautiful insects arrive in the UK. They are found in every part of the world except Australia and Antarctica.

Woodlice

Life cycle	Predator and prey	Appearance	Did you know . . .
As the weather warms, woodlice that have overwintered in homes and buildings venture back outside. This throwback to the age of the dinosaurs (they've been around in one form or another for 360 million years) has a lifespan of three to four years. The eggs hatch inside a pouch under the female's body where the young, known as mancae, stay until they can fend for themselves.	Feeding off dead plants, fungi and their own faeces, woodlice are vital to the ecology of the garden, returning valuable nutrients to the soil. In turn they are food for toads, centipedes, spiders and shrews.	Woodlice are small armadillo-like mini-beasts that are related to lobsters and crabs and have a smooth grey armour, or exoskeleton, made up of tiny segments.	There are dozens of local nicknames for woodlice in Britain, including bibble-bug, chucky-pig, roly-poly, monkey-pea, Johnny-grump, cudworm and chisel-hog. In all nearly 200 different names have been recorded.

Of course I can't mention insects without including the humble bumblebee. It's no surprise to me that whenever there's a poll on Britain's favourite insect, the buff-tailed bumblebee comes out on top. They're big, almost bumbling characters, which bob and weave in the air on their never-ending mission to find nectar. The buff-tailed bumblebee has developed an ingenious way of getting hard-to-reach food: if it flies to a flower that's too deep for its tongue-like proboscis, it will just bite a hole in the base and suck the nectar out that way. Watching them is mesmerising and apart from the crucial role they play in pollination, fertilising flowers to produce food, I suppose the appeal of these particular bees lies in their large furry rear ends and the buff-coloured 'tail' of the queens (the worker bees have much more run-of-the-mill white tails).

The females hibernate in winter and are the first bee species to emerge in early spring. They get to work straight away finding underground nesting sites, perhaps in old mammal lairs, building new colonies and laying their eggs.

Their behaviour in spring and summer is very similar to the wasp. The worker bees (non-breeding females) hatch in late spring to care for the queen, maintain the nest or forage for pollen, and it's not unusual for a colony to contain five hundred workers. Only later, in summer, will the queen produce male offspring and new fertile females to ensure the next generation and guarantee the future of the species. When a male has successfully mated with one of the new queens, its job is done and it will die. As autumn approaches the old queen and the workers also die, leaving just the fertilised new queens to find a place to hibernate. Some recent research has discovered that resting is a vital part of the queen bee's life, followed by a short burst of activity, sometimes staying on the ground for thirty minutes or more. So if you see a buff-tailed bumblebee which looks like it's in trouble, it might just be a queen resting. But if there are obvious signs it's struggling and it hasn't flown off after forty-five minutes, try moving it (carefully) to a nearby nectar-rich flower or give it a one-off energy-boost. White sugar and water in a 50/50 mix, offered on a teaspoon in a sheltered spot, will be enough to give a stricken bee the boost it needs to get in the air again. Don't be tempted to use brown sugar or honey, though – brown sugar contains molasses which is toxic to bees and honey could spread pathogens (or germs) and do more harm than good.

We have a bee farmer at Bemborough – a very knowledgeable man called Chris Wells who has been in the bee business for more than twenty years. If you accidently call him a beekeeper, he'll be quick to correct you – bee farming is a career, while beekeeping is a hobby. Chris has about thirty hives with us, and his bees particularly love a legume called Sainfoin which we grow for hay and seed. It has a lovely pink flower and the nectar is rocket fuel for bees, producing delicious honey that's very popular in our shop.

There's a wonderful tradition called 'telling the bees' which goes back so far in history that no one is quite sure how it started. It's all about the beekeeper informing the hive of the major events in his or her life – a birth, death or marriage – and there's an ancient practice of giving them some food from the wedding reception or wake for good luck. If the bees weren't told about these big life events then their keepers believed they would stop making honey, or else sting everybody in sight. It sounds like the sort of custom that died out centuries ago, but there are plenty of beekeepers today who swear by talking to their colonies. I think there's something lovely about the idea of talking to nature and wonder if we should do more to encourage this age-old habit. So next time you see a bee, pass on your news!

Now I've told you all about the birds and the bees (like a good parent should!) it's surely time to talk about something spring is renowned for: newborn animals. Plenty of species give birth in spring because of the abundance of food to keep their offspring alive and help them to grow. A glimpse of ducklings swimming behind their mother, or cubs playing around a vixen, is a wonderful sight, and even the common nouns for juvenile mammals, birds and insects can raise a smile. Some of my favourites are on the next page:

Animal	Male adult	Female adult	Young
badger	boar	sow	kit, cub
goat	billy	nanny	kid
hare	buck, jack	doe, jill	leveret
hedgehog	boar	sow	hoglet
mouse	buck	doe	pup
pigeon	cock	hen	squab
spider	male	female	spiderling
swan	cob	pen	cygnet

Nothing shouts 'spring has arrived' more loudly, though, than the sight of a newborn lamb stumbling to its feet as its mother softly bleats to her offspring. It's a scene I've witnessed thousands of times over the years, because in addition to the rare breed sheep on our farm, there's a large flock of commercial ewes. These are Lleyns from Wales crossed with Romneys which were originally from Kent, both lovely maternal breeds which lamb easily and provide plenty of milk to suckle their young. The Lleyn provides the prolificacy while the Romney has a great fleece and plenty of meat, so they're the perfect combination.

As well as retaining the best ewe lambs as future breeding stock, we also cross-breed some ewes with Dorset rams because of the excellent genetics they pass on, to produce lamb for the table. So, financially, a great deal depends on getting all our pregnant ewes through their labour successfully. In fact, every sheep breeder will tell you that lambing is the most crucial time of the year, a busy and unpredictable period of long days and sleepless nights, but if all goes well it's easily the most satisfying part of being a farmer.

The gestation period for sheep is five months, or thereabouts, and there's an old joke among shepherds that if you put the ram with the ewe on Bonfire Night with a bang, she'll give birth on April Fools' Day. We can't quite guarantee that happens every time because like all offspring, lambs have a habit of arriving when they want to. But the rest of the pregnancy shouldn't spring any surprises thanks to meticulous planning and some careful midwifery.

No one wants their entire flock to lamb at the same time. That would be chaos. So in the autumn we make sure the ram doesn't have his fun all in one go, staggering the number of ewes he services over two or three months. If you see a sheep in a field through the winter months and it has a coloured smudge on its fleece, you know it's a ewe that's expected to give birth in the spring. The stain comes from a harmless crayon in a harness that the ram wears when he is introduced to the ewes. It's called ram raddling and if we use different colours through the autumn in strict order, we can work out which ewes are due to lamb when, just by sight. It's not an exact science, but it works well enough to take most of the guesswork out of lambing time.

We also establish how many lambs are coming by scanning the ewes using an ultrasound machine – in exactly the same way that unborn babies are scanned in hospitals. With the help of a sheep race, a row of gates just wide enough to guide the ewes forward, and some good herding skills from the farmer, a really slick scan-operator can get through more than two hundred sheep in an hour.

It's normal for commercial ewes to carry twins – perfect for their two teats – but if the scan reveals just one lamb we'll spray a quick dot of non-toxic red paint on the mother's back so we're in the know when the big day arrives and we're not waiting for a brother or sister to appear. Of course triplets aren't unusual; sometimes we even see quadruplets, but the chance of quintuplets is rare. We have had more than our fair share of multiple births in recent years; several ewes have had five lambs and one even had six. They were very small when they were born but thanks to a lot of TLC, all but one of them survived. Normally a ewe produces enough milk for her lambs, but when she has three or more newborns there aren't enough teats or milk to go around, so we have to help out and bottle feed those extra hungry mouths. It's a heart-lifting thing to do – nothing like work at all – and even in a busy lambing shed at the height of the season, the volunteers are queuing up to bottle feed the new arrivals! The other option is to adopt a triplet lamb onto a ewe that has just given birth to one. We do this by rubbing the triplet lamb in the birth waters of the single newborn, so when the ewe stands up she sees two lambs that smell the same; she'll lick them both dry and is tricked into thinking she has had twins. It's different with rare breed ewes, the old slow-to-grow county breeds and primitive sheep from the wildest, rockiest parts of the UK. They're far more likely to have a single lamb because they've adapted over time to increase their chances of survival. A Herdwick ewe having a multiple birth in the wet, windswept Cumberland hills or a North Ronaldsay coping with twins in the northernmost islands of Orkney where the weather is unforgiving and the grazing is rough would struggle to produce enough milk to keep more than one lamb alive.

The signs of labour are much the same across sheep breeds, though. When the ewe becomes restless, repeatedly standing up and lying down and pawing at the ground, you know a lamb is on its way. We bring our ewes inside for lambing; it's best for the animals and means some human intervention isn't far away if a lamb is breech or a newborn needs help breathing. We also share the experience with the Farm Park visitors who sit on bales beside the lambing pens for a ringside seat as the miracle of new life occurs before their eyes. You might think people would be squeamish about seeing labour and birth at close quarters, but not a bit of it. If anything they want to see and learn as much as possible, and are keen to know all the biological and gynaecological details.

But the lambing season hasn't always been like this. For generations shepherds would stay with their flocks out in the fields through all weathers, looking over them day and night to make sure the ewes were safe and the lambs were healthy. It's why the local word for shepherds was 'lookers' in the Kent marshes, in parts of Sussex and across the Thames in Essex. Some would put up a makeshift shelter, a few hardy ones might rest under trees or hedges, but many spent their nights in wooden huts. On the treeless sweeping downs these crudely built portable caravans were easy to spot, often the only manmade structure in view with their distinctive curved corrugated iron roofs, hinged stable doors and small square windows on both sides, vital for keeping an eye on the ewes and their offspring. Most importantly these keepers' watch huts, or shepherds' huts, had cast iron wheels so they could be moved easily from pasture to pasture. By the 1950s shepherds' huts were a relic of a bygone age with many being broken up for firewood or left to rot. Now the story couldn't be more different and we've fallen in love with shepherds' huts, turning them from a humble workaday necessity into a desired luxury item; rescued huts are painstakingly restored and new ones are being bought faster than they can be built.

I don't know any shepherds who've invested in one but there are thousands being used as holiday lets, workshops, garden offices and 'man caves'.

One of the delights of the season is sitting down to a roast leg of spring lamb with the usual Sunday lunch veg and all the trimmings. But it's also where a common misunderstanding takes place; the spring lamb that's sold in supermarkets and butchers' shops in time for the big family meal at Easter or Whitsun isn't the newborn lamb that's gambolling about in the green grass. That's because spring lamb is actually winter lamb. Before lamb can be sold to the butcher, it needs to have suitable body condition and weight and usually be at least four months old. So to make sure there's enough meat in the shops to satisfy demand in the spring, some farmers start lambing in December. The press love an attention-grabbing picture so when you see a photo of a cute newborn lamb in the morning paper just after Christmas, it won't be an unusually early arrival; instead it's a perfectly timed spring lamb.

Dip inside the Farmer's Diary

The agricultural year is dictated by the seasons, the weather, the market for British-grown food and the natural life cycles of our livestock. Month by month, season after season, the activity in the fields and farmyards changes, and so does the kit and equipment needed to get the job done.

Not all arable or livestock farmers are carrying out the same jobs en masse. As you travel across the country, the exact time of certain farming tasks varies. For instance, spring lambing always begins earlier in the south of England than it does on the sheep farms of Scotland, because it's dependent on the arrival of warmer weather and the amount of new-grown grass for grazing. Mother Nature can sometimes be slightly off with her dates too!

The Farmer's Diary

As a general rule of thumb, here's what you can expect to see on the farm during spring:

	Arable farming	Livestock farming
March	Sugar beet is sown, an often overlooked crop which provides half the UK's demand for sugar. Spring cereal crops such as barley, oats and wheat are also planted. Liquid fertiliser is applied to potato fields and targeted crop-spraying is underway to combat weeds, pests and fungal disease.	Lambing gets under way in earnest with ewes separated into their lambing groups: single births, twins, triplets, etc. The ewes are vaccinated and the wool trimmed around their back end to make it easier for the shepherd to see if the ewe is lambing and to keep that area clean and free from blowflies when she goes out onto the spring grass. It's also time for kidding, when nanny goats give birth. The spring beef cattle sales are taking place in auction marts too.
April	The first blossom appears in fruit orchards, a much-welcomed sign of spring. In the fields, maize, linseed and vining peas are being planted.	Ewes and their new lambs are turned out on grass for the first time. It's the season for 'dancing' cows, when cattle are turned out of their winter housing and leap as they return to spring pasture.
May	Bright yellow fields mean the oilseed rape is in flower, a crop that's beneficial to farmland birds, especially the linnet. On soft fruit farms the first crop of early strawberries are ripe for picking. Cereal crops, potatoes, peas and sugar beet are checked for pests and protected if required.	One of the big tasks of the year begins – sheep shearing. The lambs are all safely delivered, but we're not finished with the new arrivals yet because now we're straight into the calving season. It's time for the big spring clean in the livestock buildings; all the muck is removed to heaps on the edge of the fields for spreading later in the year and sheds are thoroughly cleaned and repaired.

2

Walking in Spring: the Hedgerow

Throughout this book, at the start of each season, I'm offering ideas for spotting new and exciting things when you're out on a walk in the country. My first suggestion is the hedgerow – something we can be guilty of passing by without a second thought, but a habitat that is bursting with life.

The hedgerows of Britain are literally living history. Some are hundreds of years old, a few date back to the Middle Ages, and the oldest on record, Judith's Hedge near Monk's Wood in Huntingdonshire, is nine hundred years old (Judith was the niece of William the Conqueror and married the Earl of Huntingdon and Northampton, so she had every right to claim the hedge as her own). Hedges that are as old as the hills aren't exclusive to the countryside though; a boundary hedge in the Bristol suburb of Henleaze is at least eight hundred years old and is known, fittingly

I think, as the Phoenix Hedge. So just imagine what changes your nearest hedge has witnessed over time. When I look out across the farm at the patchwork quilt of fields stretching away to the horizon, I try to think of the stories those hedgerows could tell – the bloody skirmishes of the English Civil War, the rattling stage coach routes of Regency times and the arrival of the railways bringing smoke, steam and noise to a landscape previously untouched by industry.

Many of the hedges we see today date back to the 1700s when the old open field system and traditional rights on common land were abolished under the various Enclosure Acts. The fields were bordered with lines of trees and bushes to create individual farms. It was bad news for our farming ancestors who lost free access to the land they had cultivated, with many forced to find work in the newly industrialised cities instead. But the hedgerows which sprung up all over the country were good news for wildlife, creating a diversity of habitats and nesting sites. Fast forward to the 1940s and '50s and those same hedges were being grubbed up because the introduction of big farm machinery and the need to produce more crops to feed a hungry nation meant that working fields had to be enlarged. But more recently we've come to love and appreciate these natural borders again and today we have more than 500,000 miles of hedgerow – that's more than double the total road length of the UK and enough hedges to go around the globe twenty times!

Hedges are not only an essential part of how our countryside looks, they also play a crucial role in preserving it. Hedges keep livestock in, and protect flocks and herds from the worst of the weather. They provide another kind of shelter too – they're a wildlife habitat that's bursting with birds, mammals and insects. From yellowhammers to bullfinches, hedgehogs to dormice and bumblebees to butterflies, the thick woody surroundings and an abundance of food make the average hedgerow one great long dinner table. They act as a navigation beacon too. Bats can't get their bearings in a flat, featureless landscape so they use hedges to find their food source and their roosts. In fact, it's thought, hedges support more than two thousand wildlife species, making them one of the country's most important habitats. It's not going overboard to say they're nature reserves in their own right, so it's all the more important to make sure we don't cause wildlife loss by cutting them back too severely.

The average farmer spends a hundred hours every year managing hedgerows and I can well believe it. On our farm we rotationally trim our hedges every three years, so that two-thirds of the hedgerows are left untouched, providing fruits, berries and seeds for the birds and wildlife to live on during the winter. Untrimmed hedges and trees are signposts for birds in the breeding season, promoting their presence and announcing their territory, high off the ground. If I find a break in one of our hedges, I'm quick to make sure young hedge plants go in to plug the gap, and when the hedges get too tall we lay them to thicken them up. Hedgelaying is a traditional winter job in which stems are partially cut and bent close to the ground to create a 'living' fence, safeguarding the future of the hedge and regenerating the trees. It's a real art and can take years to master. Just ask Prince Charles – he's been hedgelaying on his Highgrove estate for decades.

The most common hedgerow trees and shrubs also include some of the most iconic plants of the British Isles. For me, the easiest tree to identify is the hawthorn; it grows pretty much everywhere in the UK apart from some parts of the Scottish Highlands. If you've ever fallen into a hawthorn you'll know it has pretty big and dangerously sharp thorns, but while they're a pain for gardeners, those needle-like spikes offer excellent protection for nesting birds and the red berries provide vital food for winter. The leaves when they appear are pale green and oval shaped, made up of several lobes on each side of the stem; but if you're unsure just look for the jagged edges. In spring the hawthorn bursts into life with clouds of sweet-smelling white flowers which have groups of long pink-tipped stamens in the middle. The fact that its white blossom appears in May is what gives it the alternative name of the May tree, and that's where the old saying 'ne'er cast a clout till May is out' originates. It's warning us not to take our winter clothes, or clout, off until the hawthorn blossom appears.

There's lots of folklore and superstition around the hawthorn, and plenty of tall tales to conjure up when you stumble across one. It's believed you should never bring the blossom indoors because it will make the family ill, or even kill them. Less terrifyingly, hawthorns were once thought to be home to fairies. In the 1200s, the Scottish poet Thomas the Rhymer was said to have met the Fairy Queen beneath a hawthorn bush, was led by her into the otherworld and only returned seven years later. The hawthorn was also the emblem of Henry VII, adopted after he defeated Richard III at the Battle of Bosworth when the last Yorkist king's crown was found hanging on a hawthorn bush.

Another tree worth looking for in the hedgerow is blackthorn. It's easy to find because it does what it says on the tin: black branches with thorns as sharp as barbed wire! Some might say the best time to visit a blackthorn bush is in autumn when the sloes appear (see page 164), but if you can catch it when it first flowers, in March and April, you'll see it without its leaves – the very dark branches on show with lots of white, fragrant blossom. Blackthorn hedges are a great place for butterfly and moth spotting, as they're a rich food source for them, and the dense shrub it creates means you can find small birds too, including nightingales and one of our rarest species, the red-backed shrike. The shrike has cleverly detected that the thorns of the blackthorn are a good natural animal trap; any small rodents that are caught become the shrike's next meal.

The wood of the blackthorn has been well used down the centuries. It was said that blackthorn made the perfect pyre for burning witches and heretics in the Middle Ages. A much jollier tradition is one which will keep Harry Potter fans happy. The Mayor of Sandwich, an old Saxon town in East Kent, is presented with a blackthorn wand when he or she is elected, a gift picked personally by the Town Sergeant from the trees that grow on the Sandwich marshes.

Next on my list is hazel. It's not as common in hedgerows as hawthorn and blackthorn, but it's still found nationwide, if a little scarce in the Midlands. Hazel was among the first species to appear after the last Ice Age and archaeologists have found hazelnut shells on the Scottish islands of Skye and Colonsay which date back to the Mesolithic period, between seven thousand and fifteen thousand years ago. Hazel is probably easiest to find before spring arrives; its long pale catkins are some of the first flowers to appear early in the year so it makes for a charming sight on a winter walk. But come spring, you're looking for tooth-edge leaves with an obvious tip. They appear in May and can be tinged with red or purple when they're young. Also have a look at the bark – unlike blackthorn and hawthorn branches, hazel is smooth and pale brown in colour. There are many lovely legends and literary references to hazel, mostly in Ireland where it was believed to be the Tree of Knowledge. The story goes that nine hazel trees grew around a sacred pool and when the nuts fell into the water they were eaten by the salmon below who absorbed the wisdom. One of the most famous figures in Irish mythology is the hunter-warrior Finn MacCool; when he was a boy, he was said to have cooked one of these fish for his master, and when Finn tasted it, the magical wisdom passed to him. So we've got hazelnuts to thank for the legendary Salmon of Knowledge.

Hazel is also one of the best trees if you're looking for mushrooms. Fungi love growing beneath hazel trees, so in the last weeks of summer and throughout autumn keep your eyes open for a large grey inedible mushroom called the fiery milkcap (so-called because a milky substance oozes from it if you break it). But one you might enjoy is the elusive truffle which grows on the roots of hazel trees. It looks a bit like black broccoli and would be one of the most exciting – and tastiest – things to find on a walk without question! Don't forget to make sure you know exactly what you're picking and if you're in any doubt, visit one of the websites mentioned in the introduction on page 13 to check.

There are other much-loved spring-time plants to find in Britain's hedgerow including:

dog rose	A lovely scrambler which clings to other shrubs in the hedge with strong curved prickles. It flowers from May right through to August and produces big pink or white five-petalled flowers with dozens of stamens forming a circle at their hearts.
cow parsley	Usually associated with roadsides in spring, this familiar hardy wildflower will grow anywhere that's sheltered. In April, May and June it puts on a stunning show of tiny white blooms which grow in clusters. It's sometimes called Queen Anne's Lace, from the legend that it burst into flower for Queen Anne and her ladies-in-waiting to reflect the fragile white lace they were wearing.
herb-robert	It's a name that's hard to forget and while it's a problem when it takes hold in a neatly tended garden, its bright pink star-shaped flowers and reddish stems add another dash of colour to the hedgerow. It's in bloom from spring right through the summer and it's long had a place in the herbalists' medicine cabinet, used for centuries as an antiseptic and a treatment for stomach aches and nosebleeds.
rough chervil	A member of the carrot family, although you would never know. It's easily mistaken for late-flowering cow parsley and it has very similar leaves and tiny white flowers. But it doesn't dominate its environment like cow parsley and will happily grow in the sun as well as in shade. Look at the stem – if it's rough and red-coloured, it's rough chervil.

hedge
bindweed

A pest or a pretty wildflower, depending on your point of view, this fast-growing climbing plant is familiar in gardens, woodlands and on riverbanks as well as in the hedgerow during spring. It has large arrow-shaped leaves and from June until September the big trumpet-shaped white flowers help distinguish it from its cousin, the pink-and-white-striped field bindweed.

In some places in the country, however, dry stone walls are more abundant than hedgerows, and it might come as a surprise to learn that they can support a wide range of plants, birds, reptiles, insects and mammals too. Dry stone walls are built without mortar or cement and have a long history in the British Isles, with the first ones appearing in the Bronze Age. The oldest surviving examples are at Skara Brae in Orkney, the remains of a Neolithic village that's five thousand years old, although most of the walls we see today were originally built in the eighteenth and nineteenth centuries at the same time that hedgerows were planted to enclose open fields and common land.

I see beautifully maintained Cotswold dry stone walls every day; they skirt the fields of our farm and line the roadsides in all directions. These well-established walls make practical barriers to livestock and handsome borders around homes, gardens, playing fields and churchyards from the southern end of Warwickshire all the way to the northern tip of Somerset. Across the entire region there are more than four thousand miles of dry stone walls, stretching out across the gentle hills and up the slopes of the river valleys like long, bony fingers reaching for the horizon.

Unlike brick and concrete, a dry stone wall isn't a solid barrier, which is a clue to their longevity. When heavy rain causes run-off from the fields, or flooding saturates the land, the space between the stones and small gaps at the foot of the walls allow water to pass through without overwhelming the stonework. In some regions, particularly in the north of England, there are even bigger gaps which look like doorways, and I suppose in a funny way that's exactly what they are. These 'cripple holes' are designed to allow some farm stock to be moved from pasture on one side of the wall to the other. They're just big enough for a sheep or a working dog to get through but too small for cattle and horses. It's why they're also known as 'sheep creeps'.

At first glance dry stone walls don't appear to add much to the biodiversity of a field, farm or village, but a closer look can reveal a habitat that teems with wildlife. Mosses, lichen, ferns, pennywort and cranesbill can grow on or between the stones while the gaps and crevices give protection to all sorts of small mammals such as field mice, stoats, voles, shrews and even hedgehogs. Frogs, toads, slow worms, bees and wasps are often found, millipedes and woodlice take refuge in the damper nooks and during the day slugs and snails will retreat into walls. The cavities in dry stone walls also provide great nesting sites for birds including wrens, pied wagtails, wheatears and little owls.

When old walls collapse it's common to find ordinary everyday objects wedged in among the stones. These tiny treasures were left by the original builders or by repairers called in decades later. Many wanted to leave behind something of themselves for future generations to find, like a kind of working man's time capsule. But others used the wall they were building as a place to hide rubbish. Clay pipes, bottles, coins and chicken bones are the most common finds, although a few years ago a pocket watch was discovered in a wall on the Blenheim Estate in Oxfordshire and I've been told about a pair of antique pistols that were hidden in a wall in the south Cotswolds. Who knows what the story was behind that! It's clear there's a lot going on with a dry stone wall, so take time to have a good look the next time you pass one.

A weed by any other name

When do weeds begin to sprout? You can't pin it to a specific date; it's simply when the soil warms up enough to prompt growth, normally around 4°C/40°F and that happens in early spring. Cultivated plants need a little more warmth to get going, which is why weeds always take hold before anything else in the garden has even started.

I've often heard wildlife lovers say that a weed is just a wildflower in the wrong place and there's a lot of truth in that. Even in farming, what was considered by one generation as an invasive pest can be thought of as a valuable contribution to the local ecosystem by the next. The cornflower is a great example. When my dad and his farming friends were young, it was a weed that you really didn't want to see growing in the arable crops, where it could easily outpace wheat, barley and oats, attract destructive insects and compromise the harvest if left uncontrolled (before farming became mechanised, agricultural labourers complained that cornflower blunted their sickles). But today these dazzling blue summery flowers are encouraged in field margins and deliberately sown in wildflower meadows. I like to think we've now got an altogether healthier attitude towards the wild plants that grow around us, and it's all about getting the right balance (and making sure the plants we want grow in the proper place, of course). There's another side to weeds that's easily forgotten, and that's the numerous ways they can be used in the home and the kitchen, or to give a helping hand to other wildlife. Here are a few weeds with lives and histories which might surprise you:

stinging nettles	Whenever I see 'stingers' on the grass verge or blocking a footpath the memories flood back of being a little boy in short trousers and the dread of being stung on the leg. It makes me feel itchy just thinking about it. I still give them a wide berth now, but at least I can appreciate them as havens for wildlife. They attract ladybirds which feed on the nettle aphids and draw in other insect eaters such as frogs, toads, hedgehogs and shrews. A clump of nettles is a banquet for moths and benefits all sorts of butterflies too, especially the caterpillars of red admirals, peacocks and small tortoiseshells. Then in the late summer, stinging nettle seeds provide food for chaffinches, bullfinches and house sparrows. Nettle leaves are good for us too – full of iron, calcium and magnesium, and tasty in a soup or a stew as a substitute for spinach. Nettle leaf tea is popular again and there's even a revival in making stinging nettle beer, or as someone I know calls it 'homebrew from the hedgerow'. Small boys with bare knees might not like nettles much, but the sting's not the only thing!
thistles	Think of thistles and we immediately picture the prickly purple plant that's been the emblem of Scotland for centuries. It certainly looks impressive on official badges, flags and insignia but it's less popular if those porcupine-like spikes get stuck in your hand. It's not the only thistle to think about, though, because there are at least fourteen species which grow wild in the UK: the creeping, spear, woolly and marsh varieties are the best known and they're popular with foragers too. All our native thistles are edible and once the spines and the tough outer layer of the stalks have been stripped off they can be roasted or braised, used in salads and pickles, and as members of the globe artichoke family, they can be cooked and eaten in the same way.

dandelions | Easily one of our most recognisable springtime wildflowers, the brilliant bright yellow flower heads are made up of closely packed florets. Break the stem and a milky sap runs out, but the biggest joy comes when the dandelion fruits and the seeds appear as fluffy fairy-like balls which fall apart and float on the breeze. As kids my sisters and I would try to blow all the seed heads off in one puff. It wasn't easy but whoever succeeded was allowed to make a wish. Some say dandelions are a useful addition to the kitchen, and the medicine cabinet too, as they're believed to be good for blood pressure, inflammation and the immune system. We've all heard of dandelion wine, dandelion tea and even major supermarkets sell dandelion and burdock (a fizzy drink version rather than the herbal variety). The young leaves can be eaten raw or cooked, the flower buds can be pickled like capers and the fresh petals are pretty versatile as well in making jam, marmalade and jelly, while the root is sometimes roasted and ground to create an alternative to coffee.

3

May Day

Throughout this book, I've recommended seasonal celebrations which I think we should revere, refresh or revive. Days linked to the seasons have been commemorated throughout history in Britain, Ireland and around the world, and the reason is straightforward enough. Until the Industrial Revolution, the majority of people lived in the countryside and the seasonal nature of farming dictated the year. Often the feasts, festivals, high days and holidays were linked to important Christian dates, further cementing them in the lives of country folk. While only a small minority of the population work the land today, and fewer people observe religious festivals and saints' days seriously, the special occasions which used to be universally known continue to sit, often unnoticed, on calendars or as a footnote in yearbooks and journals just waiting to be rekindled. They could be red letter days for a new generation, recognised as a great way to mark the seasons, connect with nature and bring communities together. Who doesn't love an excuse for a party, breaking bread with friends and maybe sharing a drink or two? If it gives us another reason to support rural businesses, food producers, farm shops and country markets, even better.

In spring that occasion is May Day. For centuries people have sent winter packing and welcomed the arrival of the sun with festivities on 1 May, a celebration that's been known over the years as May Day and May Morn in England, Beltane in Scotland and Ireland, and Calan Mai in Wales. It's easy to work out why people living in cold northern countries like ours would want to let their hair down at the coming of spring and summer, with its promise of warm weather, long sunlit days, plentiful supplies of food and the chance to meet and mingle in the great outdoors. Today we take insulated homes, electric lighting, fridges, washing machines and central heating for granted, so it's hard to really appreciate just how difficult the cold, dark days of winter must have been for our distant ancestors and the joy they would have felt as they greeted the return of spring. The delight of the ancients evolved into a huge array of customs and celebrations by the Middle Ages, and because everyone loves a bit of a bash, those traditions differed from region to region, and even from town to town.

You might think of May Day revels as a particularly

English thing: Oxford choirs singing at dawn, under-graduates jumping in the River Cherwell and town halls decorated with spring flowers, but the Celts have a long history of rituals too. Beltane is a pagan festival of fire with bonfires lit to honour the sun and encourage the spirits to nurture the crops in the field and protect the growers and their families. The festivities start the evening before and that's very much the case at the world's largest Beltane celebration in Edinburgh which involves hundreds of performers and around ten thousand spectators in a display of music, dance and the lighting of the city's Beltane bonfire. Calan Mai, meaning the first day of May in Welsh, is very similar to Beltane with an emphasis on the spirits and fire at the heart of the celebrations which are a thousand years old or more. Some local traditions have been added down the ages: May carols were sung door-to-door; the outsides of houses were decorated with flowers and hawthorn; in Anglesey, straw dolls were made and hung near the homes of young women by their jilted sweethearts; and since the 1780s people in the coal mining villages of Flintshire have danced in the streets as a way of 'awakening the spirits of summer to ensure fertility and fruitfulness' (at least that's the explanation on the May-dancing mural in Holywell High Street)!

May Day is an occasion to look forward to in many English towns and villages too, of course. Offenham in Worcestershire, Paganhill in Gloucestershire and the West Yorkshire village of Barwick-in-Elmet are just some of the places where a towering, brightly painted maypole is the tallest, and most talked about, local feature. The maypole tradition began with the Romans, when the occupying soldiers danced around decorated trees in honour of Flora, the goddess of flowers and fertility. The trees were replaced by poles about six hundred years ago and we've been wrapping ourselves up in ribbons ever since.

Nothing controversial about maypoles, you might think, but they were once banned by an Act of Parliament. In 1644 the Puritans under Oliver Cromwell declared that they were 'a heathenish vanity, generally abused to superstition and wickedness'. It sounds a bit over the top, even for Cromwell, and I'm fairly certain that the maypole dancing I love to see at country fairs and village fetes in the Cotswolds every year is totally pure and innocent.

However, a Cotswold maypole nearly spelled disaster for me when I was ten years old. My sister Becca and I were extras in a period comedy film set in the eighteenth century called *Joseph Andrews* (starring the 1960s Hollywood leading lady Ann-Margret). The shoot took place just a few miles from home in the picturesque village of Lower Slaughter where the opening scene featured a May fair with revellers singing and dancing, and even geese waddling down to the lovely, slow-moving waters of the River Eye. Dressed as two hard-working farm hands, my sister and I had the job of riding a pair of big, wide-horned White Park oxen from the Farm Park in front of the cameras. But as soon as the music began and the other actors started skipping around the maypole, the animals were spooked and bolted with two terrified Henson children hanging on for dear life! We very nearly ended up face-first in the drink!

When cameras aren't looking, maypole dancing coincides with the crowning of May Queens at hundreds of village fairs and processions around the country, when a young woman or girl is picked to represent the season and become a local 'celebrity' for the rest of the year. It sounds just like one of those 'lost in the mists of time' traditions but, in fact, most of the May Queen customs were cemented by Victorian and Edwardian grandees, keen to create an atmosphere of 'Merrie England' at their annual village get-togethers.

Much older is the cry of 'going a-maying', heard as people headed out of the village into the surrounding countryside to gather flowers and greenery to decorate their cottages. At least that's how it started, but it soon became a euphemism for couples escaping outdoors for love making. In 1583 it didn't impress the Puritan pamphleteer Philip Stubbes very much: 'Of forty, threescore, or a hundred maids, going to the wood overnight, there have scarcely the third part of them return home undefiled.' I wonder if old Stubbes was really outraged or just envious. Who knows?

When May Day comes around there are numerous ways you can mark the occasion (maybe not a-maying, though)! Washing your face in the dew on May Morn is meant to guarantee a smooth complexion and greeting the rising sun by dancing on the summit of a high hill has become quite a trend in recent years. May Morn revels happen on Painswick Beacon in the Cotswolds, Blue Bell Hill in Kent, Box Hill in Surrey and, not surprisingly, beneath the crown of pine trees at the top of May Hill which straddles the Gloucestershire-Herefordshire border.

At all those places, you can bet your breeches that the frolics will be led by a team of Morris dancers. It's a pastime that's had its fair share of ridicule and TV comedy spoofs, yet Morris sides are thriving and new ones are being formed all the time. It's the latest version of a pastime that's at least five hundred years old and began before the days of Elizabeth I, Guy Fawkes and William Shakespeare. Morris came from the French word *morisque*, meaning a dance, and the very earliest reference to English 'moryssh daunsers' is in 1448 when a group in London were paid seven shillings for a performance. In those days the troupe would have been exclusively male, but interestingly the twentieth-century revival of the pastime was driven by women and, as long ago as 1923, membership of the English Folk Dance Society was 80 per cent female. Today Alton Morris in Hampshire is a mixed side welcoming women as well as men, and new female-only troupes are emerging all the time, including Stroud Morris and England's Glory (named after the famous matches which were made mainly by women factory workers).

I love the fact that what some people might think of as 'old' traditions are being kept alive and brought very much up to date by enthusiasts and supporters. What a shame that one of our modern Morris sides wasn't included in the cultural extravaganza at the opening ceremony of the London Olympics in 2012. If you're not sure about showing off your own fancy footwork, there are hundreds of places up and down the country where you can join in with other May Day events and celebrations, from fetes and feasts to the famous 'Obby 'Oss tradition in Padstow and Minehead where elaborate decorated hobby horses parade in front of huge crowds. Even better, you could start a new custom of your own (so long as it's decent, legal and honest of course!). Either way, you'll be following in the well-worn footsteps of our forebears going back thousands of years.

As spring steps forward and approaches the threshold of early summer, the atmosphere is perfectly expressed for me in a poem of old age. It was first published in May 1922, when the famous author was approaching his eighty-second birthday:

This is the weather the cuckoo likes,
And so do I;
When showers betumble the chestnut spikes,
And nestlings fly;
And the little brown nightingale bills his best,
And they sit outside at 'The Traveller's Rest,'
And maids come forth sprig-muslin drest,
And citizens dream of the south and west,
And so do I.

'Weathers' by Thomas Hardy

Persephone and spring

Why do we have the seasons and what drives the changes between the warmth of summer and the chill of winter? We know today it's because of the earth's orbit, but for the ancient Greeks it was all about kidnap, curses and the Queen of the Underworld.

The myth starts with Demeter, the goddess of the harvest, and her daughter Persephone. One day Hades, the god of the dead, meets them and falls in love with Persephone, dragging her back to his under-world kingdom to be his bride. The heart-broken Demeter is so distraught that she curses the earth, and gives up on her duties so the plants and crops wither, livestock dies and the weather turns to winter.

Persephone's father, Zeus, strikes a deal with Hades to return his daughter so long as she hasn't tasted any food in the underworld. Too late, he realises that she's eaten a few seeds so she can never leave for good. Instead, she's allowed to return to Demeter for half the year and goes back to Hades for the other half. And that sets the pattern of the seasons – Demeter's sorrow when she loses Persephone brings on autumn and winter and six months later when she returns, spring arrives.

Five other things to see or do in spring

1. Flower spot

The emergence of flowers after winter is one of the best things about spring and the great heralder of the season is the daffodil. The daffodil is sometimes called the Lent Lily or the Easter Lily and for good reason. It nearly always blooms and fades within the period of Lent, between Ash Wednesday and Holy Saturday. Wild daffodils, unlike their cultivated cousin, have pale lemon outer petals surrounding a trumpet that's a darker canary yellow or gold, poking out above its narrow grey-green leaves. It's also shorter than a commercial daff and when they're clumped together they point in the same direction as if the trumpets are turning their faces into the sweet spring breeze. While there are clusters of wild daffodils all over the country, the really intense hotspots are fairly exclusive – Devon, the Black Mountains in Wales and the north-west corner of Gloucestershire known as the 'Golden Triangle'. When you find them, they're a sight to behold. The Dunsford Nature Reserve near Exeter is one of the best sites, with a carpet of daffodils at the base of oak, ash and birch trees.

My mum grew up in Wales which might explain my love of rugby, but definitely means I never forget St David's Day. Although I don't really qualify to wear a daffodil in my button-hole on 1 March, I look on with admiration when Farm Park visitors from Wales come through the gates on the big day proudly displaying their national flower. Well, it's *sort of* their national flower. The symbol of Wales had always been the leek and it was such an old custom that it was thought of as 'ancient' even by the time Shakespeare mentioned it in *Henry V*, written sometime around 1599. But the Victorians always preferred flowers to greens or root vegetables (not glamorous enough) and as the Welsh for daffodil, 'cenhinen bedr' translates as Peter's Leek it seemed so obvious.

The Victorians were big proponents of floriography – the language of flowers, where certain plants have symbolic meanings. Based on colour or scent, 'birth flowers' were assigned to every month (for instance, sweet peas and daisies for April, and lily of the valley and hawthorn for May) and secret messages could be delivered by sending certain blooms to friends and acquaintances. Floriography lives on today in the red roses we give to a valentine, the white lilies at funerals and the poppy emblem that marks Remembrance Sunday.

In the language of flowers, another spring favourite – the bluebell – is considered the symbol of consistency, modesty, gratitude and never-ending love. People who wear a bluebell wreath will only be able to tell the truth and turning a bluebell flower inside-out without breaking it supposedly means you will win the heart of the one you love. The superstitions keep on coming! It's said if bluebells grow by your front door it is good luck – if an unwanted visitor appears the flowers will ring to warn you. Myths aside, the list of places to find really impressive bluebell displays is a long one, and there are two or three near my home, but among the very best in the whole of the UK is Drumnaph Wood near Maghera in Northern Ireland.

Daffodils and bluebells are flowers you might already know, but to discover more take a dedicated wildflower book and get out there to identify the ones that grow in the fields around you. You never know what you'll find. There's a rare species of wild-flower that grows on my farm which makes me feel immensely proud – and protective – every time I see it. The Cotswold pennycress is a charming name for a lovely plant which, as the name suggests, is found almost exclusively in the Cotswold hills, thriving on the brashy limestone soil and rock. For most of the year it's a fairly unimpressive, inactive plant until it begins to grow in February and March when it's easier to spot the long stem and waxy grey-green leaves. But it saves its show for spring. Its delicate snow-white flowers are at their best in April when little heart-shaped seed pods appear beneath the petals. The Cotswold pennycress is so rare, prized and vulnerable that it's safeguarded by law, and the fact it grows on a corner of our farm in a Site of Special Scientific Interest (SSSI) makes it especially precious to me.

2. Look out for boxing hares

A delightful wildlife 'spot' in spring is the hare. I'm lucky to see them fairly often on the farm because they spend their lives above ground (not in burrows or tunnels as many people think). While they're often confused with rabbits, hares are larger with noticeably longer legs and ears. Those ears are good for identifying hares in the landscape – look out for their distinctive black tips. They rest in shallow scrapes or 'forms' in the bare earth which they dig out themselves, giving just enough room to settle with their ears flat against their backs. It's also where their young are born and soon afterwards the mother will place each of her leverets in its own grass-lined scrape hidden by vegetation, returning to it every night to feed. If you see a hare zig-zagging across a field, look up because there's a good chance you'll see a buzzard hovering above, searching for a leveret to snatch. It's easy to think a lone leveret found in a field is lost or abandoned by its mother, but they learn pretty swiftly to fend for themselves, so don't be tempted to intervene and 'rescue' it: there's every chance it'll return to its form and then Mum will return to suckle it later.

Until recently it was thought that the Romans introduced hares to the British Isles. But new evidence reveals that these golden-brown, lightning-quick mammals were already here when the invaders arrived in 43 AD. The Romans certainly respected hares and used them in their art and mythology; to them they represented the circle of life and fertility, naturally becoming associated with springtime and the whole idea of renewal and everlasting life. The pagans also had a bit of a thing about hares and, for them, seeing one staring up at the moon was meant to be a sign of good luck.

But there's no doubt that one of the most spellbinding things to witness is a pair of hares 'boxing' in the early spring. If you do, you might think it's two males (or jacks) in a duel over territory, food or females – but it's actually a battle of the sexes at the height of the mating season. The fight is started by the female (jill or doe) when she's tired of being pursued by a potential mate. She rears up on her hind legs and pushes at the male to tell him off! A spectacular sight if you can get a ringside seat.

3. Find some cuckoo spit

Cuckoo spit is the delightful name for the wet frothy bubbles that mysteriously appear on the stems and leaves of plants from May onwards. It's nothing to do with coughing cuckoos (I'm glad to say), but it does happen at around the same time those lovely songsters are in full voice. Inside each blob of white froth is a juvenile yellow-green insect called the frog-hopper, or as it's sometimes known, the spittle bug. The tiny adults are unusual-looking creatures, bright green with big eyes and a blunt head, and so shy that they hop away at the faintest sign of danger (or even a friendly, inquisitive human). Take a close look at your roses, fuchsias, dahlias or lavender and there's a pretty good chance you'll spot cuckoo spit.

4. Observe the food chain

The seasons are full of the drama of life and sur-vival – the delicate balance of nature with one species dependent on the other. It's pure theatre and in springtime there's no better place to witness it than in an oak tree.

Winter moths lay their eggs on the tree and their caterpillars arrive at the perfect time to eat the emerging oak leaves (they can only feed on the young leaves). The caterpillars become the ideal food for fledgling blue tits and great tits – which is why those birds often nest in oak trees and time their egg-laying with the growth of the buds.

Scientists are studying this oak–caterpillar–blue tit food chain to understand the precise relationship between the species, and work out which creatures will be able to adapt if climate change means spring arrives earlier. When you've studied an oak tree and seen nature's balancing act with your own eyes, it really brings home the importance of nature conservation, and doing everything we can to be kinder to the planet.

5. Celebrate Oak Apple Day

If you spot a stranger wearing a spray of oak leaves in their hat or lapel on 29 May, you've found a traditionalist with a great sense of history. At one time just about everyone in the land, from lords and ladies to farm labourers, would have attached some oak leaves to their clothes, and children were even given a day off school. The diarist John Byng, describing a journey through the Hertfordshire town of Barnet, once wrote: 'every horse, carriage and carter was adorned with oaken boughs and apples'. So what was the reason for all this widespread greenery? Oak Apple Day, 29 May, is the anniversary of the day Charles II rode into London to restore the monarchy to England after eleven years of Republican rule. Why an oak leaf? The sprays symbolised the legend that the king hid in an oak tree after the Battle of Worcester in the Civil War and the oak leaf became his personal emblem. Of course, apples don't grow on oak trees, so the 'oak apple' here isn't a fruit but a gall that's created by the tiny oak apple gall wasp. These golf ball-sized growths have a rough, papery texture and it was fashionable to wear them in a posy or as a buttonhole to show support for the monarchy.

We've mostly forgotten Charlie's big day now, although there are a few places where the Oak Apple Day celebrations are alive and well. In Northampton a statue of Charles II is decorated with oak leaves, at Great Wishford in Wiltshire villagers exercise their right to gather and collect kindling in Grovely Wood, folk process through the streets of St Neot in Cornwall and in the Herefordshire village of Fownhope the locals march behind a brass band on their way to a special church service. Anyone can join in, or you could simply raid an oak tree for a few leaves and pin them on your coat.

SUMMER

June brings tulips, lilies, roses,
Fills the children's hand with posies.

Hot July brings cooling showers,
Apricots and gillyflowers.

August brings the sheaves of corn,
Then the harvest home is borne.

From 'The Months' by Sara Coleridge

Introduction

In the artists' palette of the seasons, autumn is red, winters are white and the fresh new start in spring is as green as grass. That just leaves summer, which in my imagination is bright burnished gold. The sunlight, the rippling fields of wheat, sunflower heads gently dipping in the warm breeze, a refreshing pint of West Country cider on a balmy August evening: in summer it seems that everything is golden.

It's also the season of hard, unrelenting work and the culmination of a year's planning on the farm when the crops are ripe and ready for harvesting. It's a thrilling moment for me when the first combines roll into the fields, the sound of those massive motors fills my ears and the adrenaline starts pumping. Farming is a hi-tech precision industry these days, with every step of the process – from sowing the crops to selling them on – checked and monitored by computer technology. We don't send the combines in willy-nilly either. The condition of the grain, the soil, and crucially the moisture levels have to be just right, and of course the weather needs to be on our side for the maximum yield and the best possible quality. But despite all that, I'm still jumpy until everything's safely gathered and sitting in the grain stores.

On the other side of the farm, the heady days of summer are also the busiest at the Cotswold Farm Park when tens of thousands of people will pour through the gates to meet the stars of the show – our rare breed animals. Three things are crucial when that happens: plenty of water, plenty of food and plenty of shade ... and that goes for the visitors as much as the livestock. When the long school break gets underway, the camping and glamping site will be bustling with holiday-makers too, and when I'm working late in the paddocks or doing a last check on the animals, I can hear the clink of glasses and the sound of laughter drifting over from the tents and lodges. How does the song go? Keep the customer satisfied. It's a must in this business. I'll get home tired and dusty after a long, hot day and collapse into bed, my head spinning with thoughts of farming and tourism – two industries that reach their peak in summer.

Can anything beat those long, light summer evenings when the warmth of the day seems to rise from the ground and fill the air? Just a few minutes watching the birds heading to roost, listening to the crickets' constant chirrup somewhere in the distance and following the sun as it sinks slowly out of view always puts me in a lazy, holiday mood. Work starts early again in the morning, but for now I'm on my own imaginary mini-break.

4

Look Up

If spring feels like an explosion of colour and activity right in front of us after the chill darkness of winter, summer is altogether more gentle. It flows on from spring the way a stream slips into a river, which makes it an ideal time to try to spot things that are less than obvious. If we focus on what we find when we look up rather than what's under our noses, we'll see there's a whole new world of nature to enjoy, from bubbling clouds to the buzz of insects.

Cloud-spotting is a wonderfully lazy, utterly relaxing and thoroughly absorbing way of spending an empty hour or two. It's considered a hobby in its own right; you can even join the Cloud Appreciation Society and there's nothing wrong with that. Looking for shapes and faces in the clouds isn't just a way of entertaining kids on long, boring car journeys. Once you've seen an elephant drifting slowly across the sky, a barking dog or the Queen wearing a crown in the blue above, it's impossible to stop. My old schoolteachers would say they're not surprised to hear me say that, considering how much time I spent looking out the window in class!

Since then, I've been lucky enough to soar through the air to see flat-bottomed clouds close up. When I was filming with my good friend Ellie Harrison for a series called *Secret Britain* we took to the skies above Yorkshire in gliders to get a bird's eye view of 'God's Own County'. As soon as the tow-line had been released and we were flying freely, my pilot, John, told me he was looking for some newly formed cloud. The idea was to find rising thermals that we could hitch a ride on, in exactly the same way buzzards and other birds of prey take advantage of natural updraughts. The strongest lift is found beneath clouds that are just developing, so that's exactly where we went.

It was a never-to-be-forgotten experience but as well as the thrill of the ride, there's also proper science going on up there in the atmosphere. Those apparently random cloud formations all have meteorological names and a vital role in forecasting the weather. The best-known cloud formation, and the one I remember from my glider flight, is cumulonimbus. Tricky to say, even harder to spell, but it's made up of two parts – cumulo and nimbus – and when you break down the official Latin names like this, all becomes clear ... or should that be less cloudy?

 cumulus/cumulo	In the original Latin this means 'piled' or 'heaped' and it's the perfect description of these cloud formations which resemble enormous cauliflowers or marshmallows. Children might refer to them as 'cotton wool clouds'. They occur when warm air rising from the ground is cooled in the atmosphere and the water vapour that's formed builds up. They are generally a sign of fair weather but if they grow they can produce showers.
 stratus/strato	In geology 'strata' means a layer of rock or soil, and so it follows that in meteorology 'stratus' refers to a flat horizontal layer of cloud which sits low and featureless across the sky. If you see a 'blanket of cloud', this is what's taking place and on misty or foggy days, it's simply stratus cloud forming close to the ground. These clouds are formed in calm conditions when weak currents lift cool moist air over colder land. The difference in temperature causes the vapour to condense into droplets of water creating a cloud. Drizzle or even light snow could follow.
 nimbus/nimbo	When weather forecasters talk about precipitation, they're almost always predicting dark, threatening nimbus clouds. The large grey or black clouds are caused by cooling air which creates condensation, turning water vapour into liquid. The inevitable rain, hail, sleet or snow is caused by millions of water droplets which accumulate into thick layers and the air temperature will dictate whether we get rain or something more serious.

cirrus/cirro	The word translates as 'curl' or 'tuft' and these clouds are the opposite of the puffy shapes which are the stereotypical symbol on weather maps. They're often, but not always, curled and can look like wispy cobwebs, feathers, ponytails or fish bones in the sky. You might spot them behind the vapour trails of aircraft. They look lofty but actually sit in the lowest layer of the earth's atmosphere, formed when warm, dry air rises causing water vapour to change from a gas to a solid in a process called deposition. It's this solid, in the form of ice crystals, which gives cirrus clouds a bright whiteness in the sky.
alto	Although *alto* means 'high' (as every singer knows), in the cloud dictionary it doesn't imply these formations are the highest in the atmosphere, just that they're at a greater altitude in comparison to other similar clouds. They are made up of a mixture of water vapour and ice crystals and there are two types: altocumulus (high heap) are formed when moist air pockets rise and then cool down when they hit turbulence; altostratus (high layer) are thin levels of featureless grey or blue cloud. They normally appear before a warm front arrives.

The summer months are also a great time to see some incredible sunsets and sunrises. We all know that the sun rises in the east – but that's not strictly true. The angle of the sun changes through the year, so while the sun appears in the east in spring and autumn, in the depths of winter it's in the south-east and at midsummer it comes up in the north-east.

More noticeable as dawn breaks are the array of colours which surround the rising sun and reflect off the early morning clouds. The pinks, purples, reds and oranges scattered across the sky are a spectacle worth getting up early to film or photograph. But why are we treated to a stunning light show at dawn and not at, say, midday or halfway through the afternoon? It's all to do with the distance that light from the sun has to travel to reach earth. What appears to us as simply bright, white sunlight is actually made up of a range of colours of differing wavelengths. For instance, blue has a short wavelength while red is the result of long wavelengths. At noon, when the sun is overhead, the light has less atmosphere to travel through to reach us and when it does it's scattered in every direction creating bright 'sunshine'. But at dawn and again at dusk, when the sun is low in the sky, the light has further to travel through the atmosphere. It means the short-wavelength colours struggle to reach us as they're scattered further and deflected in other directions. That leaves us with the stronger, longer-wavelength reds and oranges visible to the eye.

I'm lucky to live on high ground in wide open countryside, so I get to see some jaw-dropping sunrises and dazzling sunsets. In fact, the pink and orange-tinted sky we experience at the Farm Park on summer evenings inspired us to name some of the holiday accommodation 'Sunset Lodges'.

Here are a few more favourite places to see sun up and sun down:

- Stonehenge in Wiltshire: it's famous for the massive summer solstice gathering but the prehistoric stones are a great place to greet the sun at any time of year. Tickets for special early-morning admission are available from English Heritage.
- Glastonbury Tor in Somerset: a cone-shaped hill topped with a five-hundred-year-old church tower rising high over the Somerset moors sounds mystical – and it is. The area is steeped in the myths and legends of King Arthur and many believe that this was Avalon, the isle of enchantment.
- Arthur's Seat in Edinburgh: surprisingly close to the city's famous Royal Mile, this ancient long-dead volcano offers breath-taking views over Scotland's handsome capital and across the Firth of Forth. It's another great vantage point connected to King Arthur, this time the reputed site of Camelot.
- Slieve Gullion in County Armagh: this is known as the Mountain of Mystery, associated with numerous Irish folk tales, myths and stories of heroes and villains. Sitting in a ring of hills, it's the county's highest peak with

Armagh, Down and Antrim all in view and
even Dublin Bay and the Wicklow Mountains
visible on a clear day.

There is another spectacular display in the sky, one
that's rarer and more mysterious than sunrise and
sunset. The Northern Lights, or aurora borealis, fill
the night sky with swirling curtains of green, red
and blue which seem to dance in the atmosphere. It's
serene to see but the reason it happens is surprisingly
violent: charged particles in the solar wind travelling
at up to a million miles an hour are drawn towards
the poles by earth's magnetic field and collide with
molecules in the upper atmosphere. The colours we
see are caused by the energy on impact released as
wavelengths of light. Although aurora borealis is
active throughout the year, including summer, it is
best seen in winter when the skies are darkest, on or
near the Arctic Circle in countries such as Iceland,
Norway and Finland. But occasionally, when geomag-
netic activity is strong, the north of Scotland is treated
to this beautiful, bewitching sight.

Whether it's a staggering sunset or the awe-inspiring
Northern Lights you experience, it's likely you won't
be watching the spectacle alone. Take a look up just
after dusk on a warm summer night in the garden
or a country lane, and you might notice something
dashing past from the corner of your eye; something

silent, black and very quick. It's almost certainly a bat. I remember at school several girls with long hair who were frightened that bats would get tangled in their long locks. If that was you, I'm happy to put your mind at rest after all these years – bats are the *Top Gun* pilots of the nocturnal world with finely tuned ears, and they use a kind of biological sonar called echolocation. So relax, they won't collide with your head and get trapped in your hair. A lot of people seem to be afraid of bats – perhaps because of their link in popular culture to vampires! But I think they're misunderstood mammals – their navigational powers are, for want of a better phrase, extremely cool, and like all animals they're important to the food chain. As they eat insects – mostly midges and mosquitoes – they're basically a natural fly swatter protecting our exposed skin when we want to sit out in the garden in summer with a beer! So I hope the next time you get a brief glance of a swooping bat, it brings you a jolt of excitement rather than a shudder of fear.

There are eighteen bat species in the UK and many of them are protected by law and mustn't be moved if they make their home in lofts, barns or outbuildings – but while they might make a bit of a mess with their droppings, at least they won't cause any damage to the inside of the building or munch through any cables. Trees are important to bats, and the taller the tree the better it is at helping them navigate, acting as familiar landmarks to assist them in finding their way back to their roosts. In the summer, bats find orchards irresistible, or, rather, the insects that lay their eggs in the bark of fruit trees which provide an instant snack.

Bats can be seen flying for at least eight months of the year, when they're not in hibernation, but there's another creature which takes to the air for just a few days every summer. Ants are industrious colony-building insects, the tiny superheroes of the invertebrate world, and flying ants are even more extraordinary. Most flying ants in the UK are black garden ants which live in colonies of thousands in soil, under lawns, the base of brick walls and beneath patios. Have a look at the cracks in your garden paving and you'll almost certainly see them.

Ants live in a system dominated by specific jobs: the queen lays the eggs; the workers look after the queen, her eggs and the larvae; while the drones and princesses (males and virgin queens) are responsible for producing the next generation of ants. It's the need to reproduce which causes them to grow wings and swarm in a synchronised air display. In July or August when the weather conditions are just right and the humidity rises, the virgin queens leave the colony for a once-in-a-lifetime chance to find a mate from a different colony and start a new generation. The wings are a neat bit of evolution giving her the ability to find new territory to start her own nest. A summer swarm is made up of these large-winged queens and smaller males, and when you see them joined together it's what insect experts call, rather romantically, the nuptial flight. Although that's where the charm ends because once they've mated the queen chews off her own wings and the now redundant males die. I know what you're thinking – this would make a terrible romcom!

So why do they take to the wing in such huge numbers? First because a swarm helps protect the individual ants from predators like swifts and gulls and second, it increases the chances of reproducing because the more ants there are in the air, the greater the odds of finding a mate (or mates). It really is a case of 'the more the merrier'.

You might have heard of 'Flying Ant Day', a single moment when all ants begin swarming in unison. It's a fascinating idea, but it's not based on fact. The truth is that it's more like an ant flying season, triggered by local weather conditions, which can happen over several weeks. Nevertheless, if you see a cloud of flying ants and you can resist the temptation to run indoors, it's worth sticking around to witness one of the marvels of nature.

If watching flying ants and witnessing their nuptial flight makes you feel a bit like an amateur David Attenborough, then spotting some of our native birds will definitely bring out your inner Bill Oddie. Like

Britain's best-known birder, you can learn to identify some iconic species by sight in no time at all – if you know what to look for in the first place, of course. I've been working hard planting new wildflower patches and creating nesting sites on the farm to encourage several bird species which really need a helping hand. Here are three of them and the features to look for when you're lying on the grass, gazing up:

  skylark	A little brown ground-nesting bird with a white-sided tail, a small crest on its head and a bewitching summer song; loud, complex and full of continuous high-pitched chirps. But it's their spectacular song-flight which marks them out, rapidly soaring almost vertically to great heights (which is why Vaughan Williams' much-loved classical piece is called 'The Lark Ascending').
  yellowhammer	One of my favourite birds with a name that suits its looks perfectly; the males have a bright yellow head and belly complemented by a streaky brown back. The most likely place you'll see them is perched at the top of hedges and bushes where they belt out one of the iconic sounds of the British summer – a repeated sequence of notes which sounds like, *a little bit of bread and no chee-ee-se!* They've increased in numbers on the farm over the last ten years due to our hedgerow management and the wildlife margins around our arable fields.
  linnet	This is another bird with a melodious song but it's better known for its summer plumage. The males look as if they're blushing furiously with their bright crimson chests and foreheads. These small, slim finches build bowl-shaped nests in gorse bushes and hedges. The old music hall number 'Don't Dilly Dally on the Way' used to be called the 'Cock Linnet Song' because so many cockneys kept male linnets as pets. My grandfather, Leslie Henson, was a music hall comedian so I'm sure he must have performed the 'Cock Linnet Song' at some point!

Lovely weather we're having ...

There's an unwritten rule that if you live in the British Isles you have to be obsessed with the weather! Country folk have historically been more occupied with the prospects of a dry day or a wet weekend than anyone else because it affects farming so much. It follows that there's an endless number of country proverbs that deal with the elements and weather forecasting. Are they fiction or is there a ring of truth about them? Here are some of my favourites and what they mean.

Red sky at night, shepherd's delight,
Red sky in the morning, shepherd's warning.

This proverb is very old; it stems from the book of Matthew in the Bible: 'When it is evening, you say, "It will be fair weather; for the sky is red." And in the morning, "It will be stormy today, for the sky is red and threatening."' It's not a bad rule of thumb either because a red sky before sundown is a pretty good sign of fair weather the following day. It's down to the fact that most of our weather systems come in from the west. The redness is caused by dust and small particles trapped in the atmosphere by high pressure, an indication that good weather is coming our way. A red sky in the morning shows the high pressure has already moved east and what's following behind is likely to be a low-pressure system with wet and windy conditions. I've always known this old proverb as 'shepherd's delight' but there's an equally popular alternative, 'sailor's delight'.

> *Oak before ash, in for a splash,*
> *Ash before oak, in for a soak.*

You need to know your British trees for this one. If oak trees come into leaf before ash trees, expect a mostly dry summer (we can all cope if the rain is just a splash), but if the ash leaves appear first prepare for a wet summer. Oak leaves should start appearing from late March onwards, with ash in leaf in April and May. So is the saying true? Well, nature lovers have great arguments about it every year, but the Woodland Trust sadly insists that there's no proof it works!

> *Cows lying down is a sign of rain.*

The theory is that, being gentle good-natured creatures, cows are sensitive to approaching rain and they lie down to keep their patch of grass dry. I would love this to be true, but I can already picture the *Countryfile* weather forecasters smacking their foreheads in dismay! The truth is that cows will lie down for all sorts of reasons and if you see them tucked up on the ground, it's just as likely to mean they fancied a rest.

St Swithin's day, if thou dost rain,
For forty days it will remain;
St Swithin's day, if thou be fair,
For forty days 'twill rain no more.

We have an Anglo-Saxon Bishop of Winchester to thank for our obsession with summer downpours. His name was Swithin and he requested that when he died, he should be buried humbly. So in 862 AD that's what happened and he was laid to rest outside the west door of the old minster (near the present Winchester cathedral). But more than a century later, on 15 July 971 AD, his remains were moved to a shrine inside the building, and that's when the trouble started. Ferocious rainstorms blew in and lasted for forty days and nights non-stop, apparently a sign of the saint's anger at being moved. And so the myth began to circulate that the weather on that day set the pattern for the weeks to come. Is it true? All I can tell you is that the Met Office says there are no records of forty straight days of continuous rainfall.

Rain before seven, fine before eleven.

Plenty of early risers swear by this proverb, and it's based on the fact that weather systems tend to move quickly across the British Isles on the Atlantic airflow. So if it's pouring at breakfast time, hang on because there's a chance it'll clear by the time you sit down for elevenses.

5

Walking in Summer: Livestock and Equines

There's something like 45 million cattle, pigs and sheep in the UK in any one year. That's a lot of animals grazing, chewing the cud and snuffling in fields, meadows and pens; not to mention the horses, goats and poultry which are kept commercially, for breeding or as pets. To help you make the most of your summer countryside walks, here are some facts on what the livestock you're likely to see are doing at this time of year.

Sheep

At the hottest time of the year, ewes and rams are looking a bit bald. That's because in spring and early summer they have their annual short back and sides. There are two reasons for shearing. First, the fleece is a commodity which is sold and used for everything from knitting wool and clothing to carpets and cavity wall insulation. You can sleep on it too – the best wool is used in handmade luxury mattresses. Secondly, shearing is a health and welfare issue for the animals. No one wants to wear a woolly coat in the height of summer, and sheep are no different.

If you've ever doubted the importance of sheep farming in the UK, the figures speak for themselves. We've got 33 million sheep, producing thirty thousand tons of wool every year, and cared for by thirty-five thousand sheep farmers. So that's a lot of shearing. A single movement of the clippers is called a blow and the skill comes in removing the fleece whole, using as few blows as possible without nicking the sheep (or yourself) in the process. I don't mind admitting that I've never been all that good at shearing. I can get a fleece off in one piece in three or four minutes but that's slow compared to the shearing gangs which travel from farm to farm in the summer, many of them Australians and New Zealanders who come here to earn a living while it's winter Down Under. I once made the mistake of saying on *Countryfile* that the best shearers were from Australia and New Zealand but it didn't take shearers watching at home long to put me right and point out that it's actually British men and women who are now leading the world. In fact, there's a man in Oxfordshire who can shear ninety-seven sheep an hour. In 2021, Stuart Connor from Banbury removed 872 fleeces in nine hours to set a new world record. It was a phenomenal achievement with Stuart's efforts raising thousands of pounds for charity along the way.

We've got around five hundred adult sheep which need the wool off their backs every year and thankfully our livestock manager, Mike Caunter, and his assistant Ellen Helliwell are very competent shearers so we do all the work ourselves, partly because we can, but also because of basic economics. Contractors will charge about £1.50 for every sheep they shear, but the price a farmer gets paid for a single fleece doesn't come near that. You won't stay farming long if you spend more than you earn. I enjoy helping to move the sheep in and picking up the fleeces to pack into the wool bags (known in the trade as sheets). We don't shear the entire flock in one go, because for a week or two we demonstrate shearing to the public in the Animal Barn. The children love it. It's a great way to explain the process and the amazing qualities of this natural fibre. There are more than sixty different breeds of sheep in the UK, more than anywhere else in the world, which means a huge variety of fleeces in all textures, lengths and colours.

There are the hardy breeds from the north of England and Scotland, like the Herdwick and the Shetland. The fleece of a Herdwick is thick, coarse and long; it always reminds me of wire wool and although you wouldn't want a sweater made of the stuff, it could be used for matting. By contrast Shetland sheep are famous for their very fine, high-quality wool. As Shetland breeders say 'it's got lots of crimps to the inch' with no hair or kemp in the fleece and it comes in about a dozen different colours from light grey right through to black. The long-wool breeds are, unsurprisingly, renowned for their luscious fleeces and for hundreds of years the long-wool English sheep was not only considered the finest in the whole of Europe, but generated enormous wealth for the merchants who bought and sold this valuable product (although no such luck for the poor farmers who tended them). The merchants splashed their money around and that's why there are so many historic pubs called the Golden Fleece, as well as impressive town-houses and tall church towers in the places where wool was once king.

I've been a long-time supporter of British wool and I'm not shy about promoting it. I've even herded rare breed sheep through the streets of Stow-on-the-Wold for the press and TV, while wearing an all-wool British-made suit. We definitely stopped the traffic that day. We now sell all the wool from our rare and native breeds to a fifth-generation family firm called Harrison Spinks which makes a range of high quality 'Adam Henson' mattresses which are plastic free and totally recyclable. I would love it if more people realised wool's value. It's the ultimate environmentally friendly material being natural, sustainable, renewable and biodegradable. Add to that durable, flexible, flame and water resistant. What's not to love?

Where there are sheep, you will also find the inevitable – sheep droppings. You've no doubt seen plenty of them over the years: they're small black pellets, slightly angled in shape. Now, you might not want to think too much about sheep poo – but next time you or your walking buddy accidentally step in some, cheer yourselves up with this little nugget of information. A company in Merionethshire collects the dung from local farms, sterilises it and creates a mixture from the fibres which is turned into paper. Now postcards, writing sets and even wedding stationery are being made from Sheep Poo Paper.

We're also learning more about the history of the world thanks to ewe poo. In the Faroe Islands, between Iceland and Shetland, researchers have worked out that the Vikings weren't the first people to set foot there, as previously thought. Ancient sheep droppings found at the bottom of a lake have revealed that the Celts (and their woolly flocks) arrived on the islands in the fifth century AD, hundreds of years before the Scandinavian adventurers.

Cattle

There's something very soothing about the sight of grazing cattle. Just watching them with their heads down, contentedly pulling and chewing the grass, creates a sense of calm and a feeling that all's well with the world. Some old dairy farmers might even admit to nipping down to see their herd in times of stress or anxiety, and resting a trembling hand or a tired head against the back of a favourite cow. I've even heard of one farmer who would frequently nestle down in the straw and sleep next to his cattle. They shouldn't feel bashful about it because academics agree that being close to cattle can help wellbeing. The Dutch call it *koe knuffelen*, or cow hugging, and it's being promoted as a stress-busting technique in Europe and the United States. Cuddling cattle is believed to boost the feel-good factor, promoting positivity and increasing levels of oxytocin (the so-called love hormone). Scientists say the joy-inducing secret is in the animal's size, body warmth and slower heartbeat. The cows love it too, apparently. These sessions take place on specialist sites with selected animals and under strict supervision, though, so don't be tempted to hug the next cow you see! At the Cotswold Farm Park we have a lovely red roan coloured Dairy Shorthorn cow called Strawberry. During the day she lives in our animal barn and loves meeting the public, and having her neck scratched. It's a pleasure to see people of all ages interacting with the animals, particularly something as large as a cow. But we of course know Strawberry to be a very friendly cow; livestock in the fields should never be approached by strangers.

Across the British Isles, local breeds of cattle have developed with their own distinct characteristics. The shape, size and colouring vary from county to county; some have horns, others are hairy, there are beef breeds, milkers and many which are both. They were bred or evolved to suit the landscape, the weather or the food needs in their particular area. So soft, fine-boned dairy cows suited the sunny, gentle pastures of the Channel Islands while the ancient White Park, a quality beef animal with wide horns, was impressive enough to grace the parkland of the great landowners.

There are thirty-four native breeds of cattle in Britain but the cow you're most likely to see grazing in the fields, the Holstein-Friesian, originates from the other side of the North Sea. These hugely popular black and white cows produce high milk yields and account for around 90 per cent of the UK's entire dairy herd. Continental breeds like these have a long history in Holland and Germany, but they really took off in Britain in the 1970s when farmers were striving for greater production and needed a cow which gave plenty of milk.

Before the trend for continental dairy cows, the

Ayrshire was the go-to breed for impressive milk yields and five decades later they're increasing in popularity on organic dairy farms. Originally from the home county of the ploughman poet, Robert Burns, Ayrshires are handsome cattle with red/brown and white coats and an old-fashioned square body (for centuries a shape considered superior by breeders as a sign of good bone structure and strength).

Another highly distinctive Scottish breed which is now common throughout the UK is the Highland. Large ginger cattle with enormous handlebar horns and thick wavy coats, they're an incredibly hardy breed perfectly suited to the harsh weather of Scotland's mountain regions. As well as the classic red coats, look out for other colours; including anything from chocolatey brown (brindle), pale yellow, white and even black, like my very regal-looking Highland stock bull called Black Prince. I love Highland beef and I'm not the only one – it's growing in popularity thanks to its tenderness, intense taste and low cholesterol.

There are several red cattle breeds, and while at first glance some might look similar, in reality there's a wealth of diversity and heritage which separates them. There's the Sussex, often used as working oxen and has a long smooth body with a white tip to its tail; the Red Poll, an East Anglian breed which is naturally hornless (or polled) with the only white on their tail switch and udders; the Lincoln Red, which has a deep cherry-red coat and a wide flesh-coloured muzzle; the North Devon which lives up to its nickname, the Ruby Red, thanks to its deep red-brown colour; and the curly-coated South Devon, which is the largest and palest of all Britain's red cattle. Although when it comes to sheer numbers, you're most likely to see the big, beefy Hereford. By a long way it's the most common red cattle breed and famous not just for its meat but also for its familiar white face. Even cross-bred Herefords are born with the distinguishing white face, thanks to a dominant gene in the make-up of traditional horned Herefords. It's an incredibly useful marker for identifying calves.

Even more eye-catching than the red breeds, but less well known, are Belted Galloways or 'Belties'. Whatever their colour, they have a distinctive white belt around their middle, making them the most visually striking of all our native cattle breeds. As a result of that white belt round their middles, they've earned lots of nicknames – the Polo mint cow, the Oreo biscuit cow and even pedestrian crossing cattle. Despite the funny tags, Belted Galloways have a serious role to play in boosting biodiversity because they are brilliant at conservation grazing. So keep an eye out for them on National Trust land, nature reserves and managed common land where they are used to munch away at the sward, allowing wildflowers to thrive and providing all the knock-on benefits for pollinators, beetles and birdlife.

As a rare breeds farmer, and one who appears on the BBC, I shouldn't really have favourites but I have to confess that one breed has a special place in my heart. The Gloucester, sometimes known as the Old Gloucester, is a beautiful, docile breed of cattle with upswept black-tipped horns, a deep mahogany coat and an unmistakable white stripe right down its spine all the way to the end of its tail. The trait is known as a finch-back and it's seen in other breeds, but none is as distinctive as the Gloucester. In my opinion, there are fewer finer sights than the sheen of a Gloucester's lustrous coat as it grazes in the morning sun.

I adore this old English breed not just because they are lovely to look at and have such a placid temperament but also because there's a special personal connection. The Gloucester is my county breed – I'm very proud of where I come from – and what's more, my dad helped save the breed from extinction more than fifty years ago. The last herd of purebred Gloucesters belonged to a pair of elderly sisters who lived on an old-fashioned farm on the isolated Arlingham peninsula beside the River Severn. When they decided to sell their livestock in October 1972, the future of the breed hung in the balance; would the stock be sold for slaughter or maybe used for cross breeding? Thankfully my dad, some of his friends and a few fellow enthusiasts were at the auction and dug deep in their pockets to save the Gloucester. It's a tribute to them that the breed survives to this day, and, as the dear old Gloucester isn't out of the woods yet, I'm going to keep fighting for it.

Spot some cattle on a countryside walk, and you'll probably notice they spend much of their time with their heads down, eating. But what exactly is it they chew all day long?

grass	Grown straightforwardly in fields and meadows. Cattle will pull and eat grass for long periods of the day. Just as we like variety in our diet, so too will cows be happier and healthier if the pasture also contains a good mixture of wildflowers.
hay	This is sun-dried grass. Making decent hay requires at least four or five dry days, so the old saying about making hay when the weather is fine and warm is spot on. It's then processed by a machine into rectangular bales for ease of storing and transporting. Hay is not to be confused with straw bales which look similar but are a by-product of the harvest. Straw is the dry hollow stalks of the wheat, barley or oat crop and once baled it's mostly used for bedding in livestock sheds.
silage	Pickled grass. The grass is cut and then left for a day or so which allows it to wilt. It's chopped and compacted before being wrapped in huge sheets and weighed down to keep oxygen out. It's an excellent way of preserving grass for cattle to eat later in the winter when fresh pasture is well past its best.
cud	Probably not what you think it is. The phrase 'chewing the cud' is very popular, often used as an expression for thinking something over or ruminating. Cud is actually part-digested food that returns from the first section of a cow's stomach back into the mouth for a second chewing.

Ponies

When it comes to exceptional landscapes, I think the moors of Britain are overlooked. I'm particularly fond of the two great moorland regions of the south-west – Exmoor and Dartmoor. I'll sing their praises to anyone who asks and for a horseman and rare breeds enthusiast like me, the exposed and impressive terrain is a magnet. They're also great destinations if you're looking for somewhere wild and untamed to explore on foot. So let me wave the flag for these jewels of nature for a moment and who knows, you might be convinced to take a tour or walk one of the scenic routes.

Exmoor and Dartmoor are both National Parks and I've been back to them time after time, occasionally with a film crew but often to visit old acquaintances, buy and sell some rare breed livestock or simply enjoy the scenery and the feeling of a wild, wide open space. No one can quite agree precisely what the word 'moorland' means, even though it applies to some large areas of the UK: the Denbigh Moors in Wales; Rannoch Moor in the Highlands; the much-visited Bodmin; the North York Moors – the list goes on. They all have their own characteristics, features and wildlife, and it would be a brave person who claimed that any two were alike. But broadly speaking the picture of a British moor as an open tract of uncultivated upland country is accurate, and a place that's either dry for heather to flourish, or wet with marsh and peat bogs.

Exmoor holds a special place in my heart because when I was a lad, the first breed I was allowed to look after was the Exmoor pony. They're short and stocky with a reputation for being gentle and friendly – and they are – but out on the lonely moor they are as tough as old boots. The breed is descended from the first wild horses to live in Britain after the Ice Age and that primitive quality has never left them; their feet are remarkably hard which means they never need to be shod, and they have a 'toad eye', a unique ring of raised flesh which protects their sight from the worst of the rain, snow and wind. The ponies which live all year round, in all weathers, on the moor aren't technically wild (they all have owners) but you could call them semi-feral. My Exmoors were bred from the Anchor herd which graze on Winsford Hill, a heath-covered common on the edge of the Exmoor plateau separating the valley of the River Exe from the River Barle. Far below the hill sits the most-photographed landmark in the entire 270 square miles of Exmoor National Park: a clapper bridge called the Tarr Steps, built of huge stones which act as piers for a series of heavy flat slabs weighing up to two tons each. It's mind-boggling to learn that Tarr Steps dates from the Bronze Age, making it the oldest bridge in Britain.

It's a wonderful place to visit at any time of year, but in summer there's a good chance you'll see Exmoor ponies earning their keep, grazing the heathland and preventing the purple moor grass and scrub from taking over. If you're really lucky you might even catch a glimpse of ponies splashing about in the pools and streams, drinking the cool, fresh water and playfully chasing each other over the banks.

The Anchor ponies are the largest herd of free-roaming pure-bred Exmoors in the world and they have been in the care of the Wallace family for four generations. Every year (in October, rather than summer) the current owners, Emma and David Wallace, round them up and bring them off the moor for a stocktake and a sort of equine MOT. The time-honoured tradition is called 'The Gathering' and it has another vital function – to separate the foals from their mothers so they can be weaned. It takes hours for teams of volunteers on foot, horseback and quad bikes to find the ponies and then herd them back to the farm. The first time I joined in, fog was swirling across the moor and the rain poured down – the sort of rain which manages to soak and seep through even the best waterproofs and the sturdiest boots. I was drenched. But we got all the ponies and foals in, and it couldn't have been too bad because a few years later I went back and did it again. The second time I used a motorised buggy but even then it was hard to keep up with the ponies as they shot off out of sight through the bracken and gorse.

Looking after these delightful animals and keeping the blood lines going is crucial because at one time they were on the brink of extinction. During the Second World War, the ponies' welfare was forgotten; many owners were away fighting, gates across the moor were left open and while some ponies were apparently shot for fun by troops on the moor, others were culled to satisfy demand in the wartime horsemeat shops so ended up in the pot to feed hungry families in the bomb-ravaged cities. By the late 1940s there were just fifty Exmoor ponies left. Thankfully their plight was recognised in the nick of time and today the worldwide population is around four thousand. 'We are their guardians and they are our heritage,' David Wallace told me as he checked over the mares to make sure they were fit for another year in the open. 'If we manage them properly then they are going to be here for generations to come.'

Despite the occasional foggy downpour, Exmoor attracts millions of visitors for its soft, gentle valleys and rolling hills, its greenery in summer and a stunning coastline with the highest sea cliffs in England and Wales. By contrast, Dartmoor is harder terrain; a vast grey granite landscape with rocky outcrops and tors, brooding hills, peatland bogs and valley mires. Like Exmoor it's also the ancestral home of a unique breed of free-roaming four-legged friends. The Dartmoor pony is strong, surefooted and muscular with a long mane and a flowing tail, as well as an inbred ability to withstand the wildest West Country conditions. In fact, in torrential rain and gales, a Dartmoor will face into the storm as if to say, 'Do your worst, I'm staying put.' Herds were on the moor long before written records existed and archaeologists have discovered hoof prints which go back at least 3,500 years. That heritage and hardiness was put to use in the past when ponies worked as pack animals, carrying tin and granite from the mines and moorland quarries. Then, in the twentieth century, Dartmoor prison bred its own herd which was used by the guards to escort work parties to and from the prison. Today the hardest task a Dartmoor is asked to do is to be a riding pony for children – and their friendly nature makes them excellent at it.

If you've spotted an Exmoor and a Dartmoor pony and you're hungry for more, then add a New Forest pony to your list of native equines. One of the eight rare pony breeds in Britain, New Forest ponies are semi-feral – not wild – and, like Exmoors, every one of them has a registered owner. They round up their ponies once a year, in summer or autumn, in what's called a 'drift', organised so the Commoners can check the health of their animals and gather up ponies for selling. It's also a big social event for them and a never-to-be-forgotten sight as owners on horseback skilfully and stealthily herd and cajole their galloping ponies across the heathland and into the open gates of a fenced pound. It looks and feels like a Wild West movie.

For the rest of the year the ponies have free rein in the forest and play a vital role in the local ecosystem. Their grazing of the long grasses promotes rare and wild plants like the tall, red-purple gladiolus, once called 'the gem of the New Forest', and the daisy-like bright white and yellow chamomile. Ground-nesting birds benefit too, such as the delightful long-tailed Dartford warbler, a steel-grey songster with a crimson belly which loves to perform from the top of a gorse bush. They're a precious species whose numbers crashed to just a few pairs in the 1960s. Meanwhile the southern damselfly relies on the New Forest ponies for its very survival in a few isolated spots. Sometimes mistaken for a blue and black dragonfly, the tiny, needle-thin southern damselfly is on the wing from May through to September and the female lays her eggs in the water-filled hoofmarks left by the ponies beside the lovely forest streams in the southernmost stretches of the National Park.

Together the farm and equine breeds of the British Isles are classified as 'domesticated' livestock. They were originally wild animals which were caught and tamed by the earliest farmers for a whole variety of reasons: providing meat, milk and eggs for food; wool, hair and hides for clothing and textiles; bones, hooves and horns for making tools, implements and weapons; and as draught animals, working in the fields or used as transport. I've always thought of the livestock we see around us today as living, breathing history and none more so than Britain's rare and native breeds of cattle, sheep, goat, pig, horse and pony. They weren't always rare of course, but many of them fell out of favour as farming became more intensified in the twentieth century. Every year the conservation charity the Rare Breeds Survival Trust (RBST) publishes its Watchlist of the most endangered and at risk breeds. It's worth printing it from the RBST website or downloading it to your phone and keeping it handy on your next ramble. Spotting the rarest of the rare – Albion cattle, Lincoln Longwool sheep, Golden Guernsey goats, Berkshire pigs or a Cleveland Bay horse – can be quite a thrill.

Sheepdog calls

Fans of *Countryfile* will know that every year we host the BBC's televised sheepdog trials competition *One Man and His Dog* (originally presented in the 1970s and '80s by an old friend of the Henson family, Phil Drabble). It means I have the enviable job of travelling around the nations of the UK meeting some of the best young shepherds and the most experienced flock masters in the business – and their dogs, of course. Watching them work a flock together is a joy and although I've been herding sheep with dogs for decades, I always learn something new. If you're puzzled by the strange-sounding commands the owners give their dogs or would like to learn them, here's a guide:

Come-bye – this tells the dog to move clockwise.

Away – the opposite command, to move anti-clockwise around the flock.

Lie down – doesn't necessarily mean lie down, it's an instruction to stop or pause.

Walk up – move towards the sheep.

Steady – slow down.

That'll do – the job is finished and it's time to come back to the shepherd.

You can train a dog to respond to any sound so long as it's short, consistent and distinct, but this universal language means that sheepdogs can be easily traded between shepherds. One of my friends is Dick Roper, a man who has won more titles in the sheepdog trialling world than anyone else. He explained to me that dogs don't understand the words, it's the sound and tone that matters. So the use of both is what's important, whether in a command or a whistle.

6

Midsummer

Our forefathers would have been incredibly busy at Midsummer – 24 June – because it was one of the four quarter days of the year in England and Wales when rents were due, contracts were signed and servants were hired (Scotland and Ireland's ancient quarter days fell on different dates). In fact, the custom survives because some agricultural rents are still due on Midsummer's Day and until as recently as the 1970s, local justice was dispensed at court sittings known as the Quarter Sessions.

Midsummer began as a celebration long before calendars and the written word, when the farming year was driven by weather conditions and day length rather than dates; Midsummer marked the mid-point of the growing season, halfway between planting in early spring and harvest in late summer.

Midsummer is sometimes confused with the summer solstice (the longest day and the shortest night of the year) which happens a few days earlier, on or around 21 June. I can unpack that for you! While Midsummer is about marking the height of summer with feasts, celebrations and rituals, the solstice is purely astronomical and occurs at the precise moment when the northern hemisphere is at its maximum tilt towards the sun. Of course, we're not aware of the earth's axis but we do notice that the sun is at its highest position in the sky.

There's another misunderstanding about Midsummer – that it's when fairies and spirits are at work and up to mischief – but that's thanks to William Shakespeare and his comedy *A Midsummer Night's Dream*; despite its title that play actually takes place on the eve of May Day.

Ignoring naughty nymphs and playful pixies, Midsummer celebrations began when our pagan ancestors started to notice that after the mid-point of the year the sun was weaker and the days were becoming shorter. So, on Midsummer's Eve, they lit bonfires to try to encourage the sun and call it back to full strength. In fact, the word 'bonfire' is thought to have originated because of Midsummer, when the richer folk would lay out food and drink around the fire, and neighbours would come together to celebrate; the word 'bon' – 'good' or 'boon' – was attached to the word fire.

If you live somewhere you can safely – and legally! – light a bonfire and get your neighbours together, then what a lovely communal celebration to revive. If that's not possible and you'd like to see a Midsummer fire for yourself, the West Country is a great place to start. The Old Cornwall Societies act as the driving force behind the lighting of a series of hilltop fires every year on Midsummer's Eve. From Kit Hill near the River Tamar all the way down to Chapel Carn Brea near Land's End, ceremonies take place in English and in Cornish as herbs and flowers are thrown on to the stacks of wood. Then just as the sun disappears below the horizon, the person chosen to be that year's 'Lady of the Flowers' lights the fires. It figures that the word Midsummer in Cornish is Golowan which translates as 'Festival of Light and Happiness' and the day of the bonfire lighting coincides with a torchlit procession through the streets of Penzance with the crowds following the musicians from the Golowan Band.

Festivities like that were common all over the country in the Middle Ages when the idea of Midsummer had grown to become a major event in the calendar. Five hundred years ago those Cornish bonfires accompanied by parades and music would have been very familiar just about everywhere and all sorts of greenery was brought back from local forests and woodland to decorate houses and churches. The religious side to the festival was important because 24 June is St John's Day, the feast day of St John the Baptist, and the records are full of references to him. Birch was the special tree of St John, and furnishing rooms and buildings with green birch was meant to symbolise the great saint and the gospel story of him preaching in the wilderness. So churches were decorated with birch boughs, and surviving archives from the 1400s at St Mary-at-the-Hill in London show payments for 'birch at Midsummer' every June for decades on end.

The Midsummer bonfire tradition is also strong in Scotland and stems from an old Celtic fire festival which involved blessing the crops in the fields and the livestock on the land with flame. Bonfires were lit at sundown and after a fair amount of eating, drinking and dancing, the farm animals were led around the bonfire in a sunwise direction (the Scottish folklore description of clockwise, mimicking the sun's journey from east to west). The flames were associated with the ancient Sun God and an animal bone was some-times thrown into the fire to symbolise a sacrifice in a tradition that clung on even after the arrival of Christianity in the fourth century AD.

Torches made with heather were lit from the bonfire and carried around the fields three times (in a sunwise direction again) to safeguard the crops until harvest, before the same was done around the byres and barns to bless the cattle in the hope of warding off lameness and disease. Midsummer fires were popular, espe-cially in rural areas, well into the eighteenth century and in many ways I can relate to those Celtic farmers and their efforts to please the powers on high – in the twenty-first century we're not quite so superstitious but we still do everything we possibly can to ensure a good harvest and raise a herd of healthy cattle.

At Midsummer, the Highlands and Northern Isles can experience as much as nineteen hours of daylight, which is almost two and a half hours more than London. In fact, in Shetland, the most northerly part of the UK, the sun just dips below the horizon for a few hours between sunset and sunrise. So a late evening walk in some of Scotland's loveliest locations is a must. I'm a great fan of the Scottish isles, and especially Islay off the west coast with its sandy beaches and sweeping bays which stretch along 130 miles of exceptional coastline. It's known as 'The Queen of the Hebrides' and after a family holiday there in 2021, I can recommend it as the perfect place to mark Midsummer with a sunset bike ride or a beach walk.

I don't know what's on Scotland's list of most-loved sports but I'm sure golf is near the top. So it's no surprise that the country's tourist board, Visit Scotland, suggests celebrating Midsummer by playing a round of twilight golf. There are plenty of courses where players love to take a swing as the sun begins to set. Traigh in Inverness-shire is the most westerly golf course on the UK mainland and is based on a line of grassy hills with beautiful views across the water towards the isles of Eigg and Rum. Further north,

Durness in Sutherland offers golf from dawn to dusk, with the ninth hole near dramatic cliff edges and the green within earshot of the crashing waves below. At Stromness in Orkney the seaside parkland course has an unrivalled view of the sheltered waters of Scapa Flow, where Vikings anchored their longships and the Royal Navy was famously based in the two World Wars. I'm more of a rugby man myself but I'd be very happy to tee off in the twilight at any of those heart-stirring spots.

The bonfires that were so familiar in Scotland and England were also the way people in Wales once greeted Midsummer (Gŵyl Ifan in Welsh). A bundle of charred wood from the previous year was normally used to start the bonfire on Midsummer's Eve and it was kept burning throughout the night so that dawn was greeted by flame, in praise of the sun.

There were local variations on the bonfire theme. In Glamorgan for instance, cartwheels covered in straw were set alight and rolled downhill; if they were still blazing away when they reached the bottom it was seen as a sign of a good harvest to come.

There's a less dramatic tradition in Pembrokeshire but one which, rather sweetly, still continues. Below the Preseli hills, not far from the town of Narberth, are the ivy-covered ruins of the long-forgotten parish church of Newton North. Ownership of the twelfth century landmark includes an ancient obligation to present a white rose, the symbol of innocence and purity, to the Church of Wales once a year on Midsummer's Day. No one knows why the practice started, or when, and the building has been nothing more than a shell for generations. For many years the overgrown ruins and the surrounding five hundred acres of countryside and woodland have been owned by a local business which runs the area as a holiday resort. You might think that it would be easier to let obsolete old rituals wither away in the modern commercial world – but not in Pembrokeshire. Every year without fail, the company upholds the custom by presenting a white rose to the church on 24 June in the same time-honoured way.

It's a time of the year that's laden with folklore and old country wisdom, some of which can still be heard today: 'If the cuckoo sings after St John's day, the harvest will be late' is one example. There's also a warning for weed-obsessed gardeners in a popular rhyme:

> Cut your thistles before St John,
> You will have two instead of one.

If you want to bring back some other Midsummer traditions, there are a few things you could do. First, pick some roses: there was a belief that roses picked at Midsummer would last until Christmas. I'm not sure how that one can be true but you'll never know if you don't try! Another one recommends that women looking for love should scatter rose petals in front of themselves at midnight on Midsummer's Eve and then recite the lines:

Rose leaves, rose leaves,
Rose leaves I strew.
He that will love me
Come after me now.

The following day the magic should happen and their one true love will appear.

Third, go in hunt of some 'fernseed'. This isn't actually a seed, but the small spores on fern leaves. Folk tales held that fernseed made you invisible (Shakespeare even referenced those qualities in one of his plays, *Henry IV*) and it was thought that the only night to find it was on Midsummer's Eve. Traditions about it vary – some say you need to collect it on a pewter plate and keep hold of the plate to stay invisible. So make sure you take the correct kitchenware with you if you're going a-hunting for fernseed!

Is it me or are the heady days of summer over far too quickly? I'm all for squeezing the most out of the last days of the season of heatwaves, holidays and harvest. In late August and early September, an early morning walk across the fields and down the country lanes always sets me up for the day. There's a freshness to the air and the cool shade from the high hedges is a welcome contrast to the heat of the midday sun. The first fruits of this year's apple crop are sweet and juicy while the garden and the greenhouse are full of colour with ready-to-pick tomatoes, cucumbers, gooseberries, blackcurrants, runner beans and marrows.

For me, the end of summer is when I really start to relax and enjoy the season. It's when the last of the wheat and barley is in the grain stores, about the same time as the posters go up for the forthcoming Harvest Festival in the village church. In just a few days I'll be planning the job that seals summer for farmers everywhere – preparing the fields for next year's crop. But I think I can take a few minutes to savour the moment by finishing that bottle of English Pinot Blanc and pouring a final glass. The last of the summer wine, indeed.

The Farmer's Diary

Here's what you can expect to see from farmers during summer:

	Arable farming	Livestock farming
June	Hay-making begins when the grass that's been left to go to seed is cut and dried in the sun. It's a crucial job for any farmer who needs food for livestock during the winter. Potatoes need irrigating (or watering) to grow and fill out. Salad vegetables and soft fruits such as cherries and gooseberries are in season.	It's the height of the agricultural show season so the finest cattle, sheep and pigs are primped and preened ready for judging. Dairy and beef cattle are mated in June for calving in the spring while in the sheep sheds the last of the flocks are being sheared.
July	Harvest – the highlight of the arable year – begins. Oilseed rape is usually the first winter-sown crop to be gathered in. It's harvest time on fruit farms too with raspberries, blueberries and blackcurrants ready for picking.	The best of the fattened spring-born lambs are being chosen for the table. Turkeys are hatched and sent to farms where they will be reared for Christmas.
August	If the weather is good, the combines can harvest this year's barley and wheat crop. Next year's oilseed rape is planted from mid-August.	On farms with grass and wildflower meadows, remaining lambs are weaned and are out grazing a few weeks after the midsummer hay cut (this is called aftermath grazing).

Five other things
to see or do in summer

1. Watch the harvest

A cloud of dust, a steady thrum in the air and a notice-able increase in farm trailers trundling along country lanes, well into the evening and after dark: sure signs that harvest is under way in the fields of Britain, the busiest time of year as the crops are safely gathered in. Two or three consecutive days of dry weather and no sign of a summer thunderstorm on the horizon is the signal for a mini-invasion of the arable fields as wheat, barley, oats and rye are harvested. The constant drone that can be heard in the distance is the sound of the combine harvester, or simply the 'combine' in farmer-speak, a machine we take for granted now but one of the greatest labour-saving inventions of all time. It gets its name from the fact it combines three separate jobs which until relatively recently were all done by hand: reaping, threshing and winnowing.

Reaping – the cutting of the crop.

Threshing – separating the edible seeds (the grain) from the stalks (or straw).

Winnowing – removing the inedible husk, or chaff, from the grain.

We think of harvest as an intense period which happens for a couple of weeks in mid-August, but in truth the season is drawn out with many modern crop varieties bred for early maturing. My oilseed rape and winter barley are harvested in July, spring malting barley at the beginning of August, followed by wheat later in the month, but it might be well into September before all the linseed and winter beans are brought in.

Despite the modern timetable, the harvest rituals of old live on. For centuries it was expected that the entire village would pull together to help bring the crops in, and well into the twentieth century that included children. The six-week school holiday that kids enjoy every summer is a remnant of those times; it was pointless to expect classrooms to be full of bright-eyed, attentive children when they were needed out in the fields. Two vital jobs they did were gleaning and rabbiting or ratting. Gleaning happened after the crops had been scythed and involved searching for any leftover corn that had been missed by the harvesters. If the children worked long and hard, they might collect enough to eventually make bread to feed the family in the hungry months ahead. Rabbiting and ratting was less laborious but definitely not a job for weak stomachs. It was a form of pest control and a source of valuable food: they would kill the rabbits, rats and any sort of vermin which would break cover and run out of the fields as the crops were cut. Gangs of boys would give chase with long sticks and hope their prey didn't run into a hedge or under the sheaves of corn piled up into stooks across the harvested field.

I'm not sure it's a job many children would want to revive today! But there's one pastime which just about lingers on and could well take off again. Every so often I see a corn dolly hanging up in a village hall or on display at a county show; they're a reminder of communal harvesting and I'd love to see them more often. A corn dolly is a hand-crafted figure that's woven or plaited from the last sheaf of corn from the harvest straw and hung up in a barn or farm kitchen as a good-luck charm. The old belief was that the spirit of the harvest lived in that last sheaf, so after a winter inside it would have to be ploughed back into the field after Christmas (probably on Plough Monday, the first Monday after Twelfth Night when work resumed on the farm). The word dolly makes it sound as if these figures are straw people, but they're mostly simple abstract shapes and twists, sometimes horseshoes or anchors, and there are local variations: the Suffolk bell, Anglesey rattle, Durham chandelier, Hereford lantern and Stafford knot. Although the craft is ancient, the name is relatively new – until the 1900s they were called 'harvest tokens' or 'harvest trophies'.

Harvest time was, and remains, such a pivotal time of year that dozens of songs about it were handed down from one generation to the next. Everyone knew the songs of the countryside – 'Oats and Beans and Barley Grow', 'Jim the Carter Lad' and 'The Thrashing Machine'. In the days before broadcasting, and even the earliest wind-up gramophones, the only way to hear these songs was to perform them. Many of the harvest folk tunes and lyrics weren't noted down until the early twentieth century when collectors such as Cecil Sharp toured rural counties asking elderly villagers to sing for them on their doorsteps or in the kitchen parlour. Sharp and a handful of others gathered up the fragments of the old tradition in the nick of time. Thanks to them those songs live on today. You can find all the tunes and lyrics online but for the genuine thing, nothing beats going to a folk night in a village pub or a Harvest Home supper to experience the thrill and atmosphere of a live performance.

2. Smell the rain

When the clouds open in summer and the rain pelts down, bouncing off pavements and car bonnets, it's always with a sense of relief that the weather's broken and there's a brief respite from the oppressive heat.

There's something soft about summer rain when it hits your face and instead of screwing my eyes up, like I do when I'm caught in a winter downpour, I turn my head up towards the sky and let the water cool my skin. After days or even weeks of dry weather, a sudden storm in summer creates a unique refreshing smell, taking the dust out of the air and drawing evocative natural odours from recently mown grass and newly planted flower beds.

The smell of rain has a proper scientific name, believe it or not. It's called petrichor, a term that was coined only in 1964 by two Australian researchers who discovered the scent was created when an oil secreted by plants in dry weather was combined with chemicals released by soil bacteria. If you've ever thought you could 'smell rain on the way' – you can. That's because higher humidity just before a cloudburst triggers the release of small amounts of the oils from rocks and soil. But the full effect is reserved for rainfall which causes minute air bubbles on the ground which burst through the individual raindrops, throwing tiny particles of scent through the atmosphere and away on the breeze. If only I could bottle that smell I'd make a fortune!

3. Go to a lavender field

In summer, the light, fresh floral scent from the long purple blossom of lavender is on the breeze, reminiscent of a woodland floor smothered with herbs and grasses. While lavender grows in all four corners of the UK and we think of it as a native plant, it is, in fact, originally a Mediterranean shrub with a long history. When the tomb of the Egyptian boy king Tutankhamun was opened in 1922 by the archaeologist Howard Carter, he found traces of lavender and the scent could still be detected.

Yorkshire, Norfolk, Kent and the Cotswolds are among the places where lavender farms are part of the summer tourist trail and there's a healthy commercial market for English and Scottish lavender. If you do visit a lavender field, you might be wise not to embarrass yourself by singing the famous lavender song out loud. When I was at agricultural college in the 1980s one of our favourite rock bands was Marillion and they had a big hit with a song called 'Lavender' in 1985. What we didn't realise was that it was based on an old English folk song (I think a few of my old college mates would have been horrified at the time, frankly). 'Lavender Blue' is a love song that has been around since the 1600s, and a saucy one at that, but it was made respectable and by 1805 it was published as a popular nursery rhyme:

> *Lavender blue and Rosemary green,*
> *When I am king you shall be queen;*
> *Call up my maids at four o'clock,*
> *Some to the wheel and some to the rock;*
> *Some to make hay and some to shear corn,*
> *And you and I will keep the bed warm.*

4. Find the hummingbird hawk moth

There's something like 2,500 species of moth in the UK and many of them are genuinely beautiful, if you can get close enough to see them properly. But for me the most exciting and unusual variety is the hummingbird hawk moth.

It really does look like a hummingbird with a thick-set brown and white spotted body, orange hindwings and most bird-like of all, large round eyes. It behaves in the same way as its exotic namesake too. It hovers in front of nectar-rich flowers like honeysuckle, jasmine, lilac and buddleia and unfurls its long proboscis to drink in its sugary fix before darting off to the next bloom. When it's on its aerial mission the wings become an orange blur and beat so quickly that they make a hum – just as the name suggests. It even appears to have tail feathers like a real bird. Moths are normally night-time fliers but there's no need to stay up late to catch the hummingbird hawk moth because it's on the wing during the day; in fact, it prefers bright sunlight which is lucky for us. From June through to September keep your eyes open for one whizzing around flower gardens, farmland, woods, meadows and coastal countryside. At one time or another they've been spotted in every county in the UK from Cornwall to Caithness and even out to Orkney and Shetland. They breed here but our winters are too cold to survive, so they migrate back to southern Europe when autumn arrives.

5. See Swan Upping

It's a strange phrase, Swan Upping, but it's a uniquely English tradition and I always think it has a whiff of *Three Men in a Boat*. Just like Jerome K. Jerome's famous book, it takes place on the River Thames in summer and is guaranteed to attract fascinated spectators and awe-struck schoolchildren on the banks and on the water. It's basically an annual census of the swans on the river and it's full of colour and pageantry. The swan keepers of two famous livery companies in the city of London, the vintners and dyers, travel upstream from Sunbury to Abingdon in small wooden rowing boats, or skiffs, catching and weighing all the swans and cygnets they find. With flags fluttering in the breeze and the cry of 'All up' when they spot a family of swans, the Uppers are accompanied by the Queen's Swan Marker who is unmissable in his scarlet uniform jacket with gold braid and trim, smart white trousers with razor-sharp creases and a captain's hat adorned with a large white swan's feather (usually perched at a jaunty angle).

When this spectacle started nine hundred years ago, the kings and queens of England would feast on royal swans. Thankfully these beautiful birds have been off the menu for a long time now, and today Swan Upping is about animal welfare, conservation and education.

AUTUMN

Warm September brings the fruit,
Sportsmen then begin to shoot.

Fresh October brings the pheasants,
Then to gather nuts is pleasant.

Dull November brings the blast,
Then the leaves are whirling fast.

From 'The Months' by Sara Coleridge

Introduction

The dazzling display of colour in the trees as the leaves put on a spectacular show can mean only one thing: that autumn has arrived. Leaves that were green a few weeks before now burst into glorious shades of red, yellow, orange, purple, gold and even pink. It's all down to chemistry. As the days shorten and the weather turns colder, leaves stop producing chlorophyll, the pigment that gives plants their green colour and helps them absorb energy and obtain nutrients from the sun. As photosynthesis shuts down, the other natural colours that were present all year, but masked by green during the summer, are finally revealed. If you're in a wood or forest and you hear a ranger or a tree surgeon mention 'full tinting' they mean the tree has completely changed colour and all the green leaves have turned.

In North America the annual pilgrimage to the states of Vermont, Maine and Massachusetts has been called 'leaf-peeping' for decades, and the New England tradition has now crossed the Atlantic to Old England! You can now join other leaf-peepers on treks and tours through Grizedale Forest in the Lake District, Cardinham Woods near Bodmin in Cornwall and in the Forest of Dean and Wye Valley where England and Wales sit side by side. In fact, the UK's first official leaf-peeping driving trail opened at Symond's Yat, overlooking the Wye, in 2019 with the launch of a fifty-mile route through one of the country's most picturesque regions and one populated by 20 million trees of two hundred different species. The hope is that the area will become the nation's 'leaf-peeping' capital. Great news for local hotels, cafés and shops I'd have thought.

One of my favourite things about autumn takes me on a trip down memory lane: it's conker season! My old school in Cheltenham was surrounded by horse chestnut trees and I used to spend hours looking for the biggest, toughest, shiniest conkers I could find. I had a scarf that I turned inside out and filled with as many conkers as I could carry, then I'd head back inside and tip them all out into my locker. I took enormous pride in picking the best specimens, drilling a hole through the middle with the compass from my geometry set and threading it with a bootlace.

If you've never had a game of conkers, it's straight-forward enough. Two players take it in turns to hit, and eventually destroy, their opponent's conker. The winner's conker then becomes a 'one-er' and if they beat the next contender it becomes a two-er, and so on. Did I ever soak my best conkers in vinegar, bake them in the oven or put cement in the middle to give them extra clout? That would be telling! But I can reveal that apart from providing top-level sport (for under elevens), conkers can save your winter ward-robe and keep you clean. As conkers dry out, they release a natural moth repellent and popping a few in the pockets of your jacket or coat might be enough to ward off an attack by hungry moths. And it was the Vikings who discovered the benefits of horse chestnut soap. They soaked and crushed conkers to make soap, which worked wonders thanks to naturally occurring chemicals called saponins that are still added to some shampoos and shower gels today.

Aside from trees and conkers, there are so many things to enjoy in autumn, as I hope the following pages prove.

7

Welcoming Old Friends and New

Autumn is the season when migrating wild-fowl flock to our shores to overwinter. There is something timeless, reassuring and reliable in the knowledge that whatever else is going on in the world, a magical combination of genetics, instinct and flock behaviour will kick in, come what may. It compels huge numbers of beautiful geese to undertake heroic journeys which bring them right to our doorstep. After a summer spent in places like Siberia, Canada and Greenland, they seek warmer climes and a return to familiar feeding grounds within the UK such as estuaries, marshland, gravel-pits, lakes and reservoirs. If you come across them en route you're likely to hear them before you see them, because the brash, noisy visitors make their presence known with loud honks. If you look up, you'll see their satisfying symmetrical V-formation, called a skein, which is vital in order to conserve energy. The leading bird breaks the wall of air in front of the skein and then each goose in turn 'rides' the minor turbulence created when air passes the wings of the one in front, giving it a slight lift. The honks are from the geese at the rear encouraging the lead birds to keep the pace up – they are the back-seat drivers of the wildfowl world.

Among the annual visitors are about sixteen thousand white-fronted geese which descend on the Severn estuary in Gloucestershire, the Swale estuary in Kent and the west coast of Scotland every autumn. Bigger than a duck and smaller than a swan, this grey-coloured bird gets its name from the white patch on the front of its head around the beak. In fact, the beak is the tell-tale clue to where an individual white-fronted has flown in from: Siberian birds have a pink bill while the Greenland white-fronted has an orange bill – nature's version of stamps in a passport!

One of the easiest geese to identify is also one of the smallest. The brent goose is another Siberian arrival but differs from the grey goose breeds thanks to its dark plumage – a distinctive black neck and head with a grey-brown back and a pale or dark belly, depending on the breed. Its name, brent, comes from the old Norse word 'brand' which means burnt and was an early description of the bird's colour, looking like charcoal. The brent loves saltmarsh and estuaries and its favourite over-wintering grounds are in the east of England. So for the best sightings head to the Rivers Blackwater, Crouch and Roach in Essex and the Thames estuary. The Essex Wildlife Trust reports that a quarter of the world's total population of dark-bellied brent geese spend autumn and winter on the county's coast after their epic 2,500-mile migration. Norfolk's coastal marshes and The Wash are good spots too, and if you go bird-watching in East Anglia two years running, there's a good chance you'll be seeing the same birds because brent geese pair for life, migrate in family groups and return to the same grounds every year.

At the opposite end of the scale is the greylag, the biggest and bulkiest migratory goose and the grand-daddy of the gaggle as it's the ancestor of almost all domestic geese. The grey plumage is topped off by a distinctive short orange bill and pink legs, and they waddle and peck with a dignified air, but their call is anything but. It's a loud, nasal cackle that's impossible to ignore. If you were brought up on the nursery rhyme 'Goosey Goosey Gander', well, that was a grey-lag, according to historians (although I'm not sure how they know). These days the genuinely wild greylags can only be found in Scotland and they're joined by thousands of others from Iceland every year.

But for a truly dramatic story of international migration on the wing, look not at geese but to the Bewick's swan. The smallest swan in the UK, it's named not after a place but a person: Thomas Bewick who was an eighteenth-century illustrator from Northumberland with a gift for engraving birds and animals. Hardly anyone has heard of him, but his intricate artwork impressed William Wordsworth, Charlotte Brontë and Alfred, Lord Tennyson so much that they all wrote poems or tributes about him. He's even got a second bird named after him – Bewick's wren. Thomas was obviously an impressive fella and so I hope this helps to put him on the map.

The astounding thing about Bewick's swans is their black and yellow bills; the pattern of each bill is unique to the individual swan in exactly the same way that fingerprints are to humans. Since 1964, exact bill patterns for migratory Beswick's coming here have been drawn and recorded with each swan given a name. It means they can be identified year after year, and in some cases decade after decade, as they visit the same wintering grounds. It's the bird world's equivalent of a number plate.

Britain's Bewick's swan capital has to be the wild-fowl reserve at Slimbridge on the banks of the Severn estuary in Gloucestershire, a place that's been called the birthplace of modern conservation and described as an avian Serengeti. Sitting on the flat plain that stretches along the lower east bank of the UK's longest river before it merges into the muddy waters of the Bristol Channel, Slimbridge is a small farming village.

Converted farmhouses, old barns and cattle sheds line the narrow road that runs through the village and twists between the fields on its way towards a single-track swing bridge over the Sharpness canal. In 1946 the Severn Wildfowl Trust opened its first reserve about half a mile further on, where the land meets the estuary in a marshy, flood-prone area called The Dumbles. Since then the organisation has been renamed the Wildfowl and Wetlands Trust (WWT) and the word 'Slimbridge' has become international shorthand for world-class research, vital breeding programmes and the largest collection of captive wildfowl on the globe. I would definitely recommend a walk out to the bird hides overlooking the salt marsh or a trip up the viewing tower to appreciate how the lagoons and reed beds sit within the dramatic open landscape. Unlike many open-air attractions, WWT Slimbridge is at its best in the late autumn and winter when around thirty thousand ducks, geese and swans are feeding and roosting on the wetlands. It's a visual spectacle but delightful on the ear too, with the air filled with the sound of birds of every shape and size chirping, tweeting, quacking, honking and hooting!

If Slimbridge feels like an international arrivals lounge of the bird world, then gardens and open farmland are the departure terminals. As wildfowl fly in from the north, many smaller birds begin their long autumn journeys following the sun south.

In late summer I love to watch swallows fluttering about, swooping across the garden, looping the loop above me or perching in little flocks on telegraph wires like a row of tiny soldiers on parade. That high-wire balancing act is the perfect moment to see their long forked tails pointing to the ground below. The swallow is a small bird, about the size of a matchbox, with metallic blue feathers, a pale underside and a flashy red throat. Their arrival here is eagerly awaited as a famous sign of spring, but I've always thought that when they leave, the call goes out that autumn is definitely on its way. They eat flying insects, flies and bluebottles mostly, which they catch in the air so warm weather is vital for survival. As the days shorten their natural instincts kick in and they'll be off on a staggering six-thousand-mile migration to South Africa, covering anything up to two hundred miles a day.

Another migrant which overwinters in Africa is the little ground-hopping member of the chat family, the wheatear. Flying at night and stopping to feed and refuel in North Africa, it spends four or five months in Senegal, Sierra Leone, Kenya or Mali before making the reverse journey to arrive back here in March. About the size of a robin, wheatears have black cheeks and a delightful orange blush on their breasts. The name has nothing to do with ears of wheat; instead it comes from the old English words for white (wheat) and arse (ear) which is exactly what they have! In the 1700s they were a popular snack. It's hard to believe now but in seaside resorts on the south coast half a million wheatears were caught and roasted every year. The wheatear season started on 25 July and some switched-on shepherds in Sussex supplemented their low wages by selling birds to visitors for a penny a time. Nowadays the idea of trapping, plucking and eating wheatear on a spit is pretty distasteful as well as being illegal. And quite right too.

One species I'm doing my best to encourage on the farm is the turtle dove. Romanticised by poets, folk singers and musicians and mentioned many times in the works of William Shakespeare, the words 'turtle dove' really do mean love (in cockney rhyming slang at least). This delicate-looking bird with its pink chest and orangey-brown back is another long-distance traveller. It leaves us in September for sub-Saharan Africa, travelling at speeds of more than 30 miles an hour and able to cover four hundred miles at a time without stopping.

But perhaps the most remarkable migration story is that of the puffin. These small black and white birds with colourful orange and yellow bills are almost comical as they hop, waddle and totter about and it's easy to see why they're called 'the clowns of the sea'. There are a few mainland colonies; Bempton cliffs in Yorkshire and a collapsed sea-cave called the Bullers of Buchan in Aberdeenshire spring to mind. But most UK puffins live on islands around the coast – the best known are Skomer, Pembrokeshire; Rathlin Island, County Antrim; the Farne Islands, Northumberland; and the Isle of May, Fife.

After spending months on the cliffs and rocks, breeding and raising chicks, the puffin returns to open water once more in the middle of August. We won't see them again until April when they come inland to the same breeding site – a hole or burrow in the ground or cliff side – to be reunited with their mate, as they spend the entire autumn and winter on the vast ocean, diving deep underwater and feeding on fish. Until recently it was thought many of the puffin colonies which nest down the east coast ventured out over the North Sea, but electronic tagging has revealed that most of them head for the open waters of the North Atlantic instead.

While we wait for our feathered friends to return, we can ponder on the new 'friends' being made down on the ground. Autumn means mating time for one of our most iconic wild animals. Britain's biggest land mammal, and our largest deer species, is the mighty and magnificent red deer. This is the monarch of the glen, the Exmoor emperor, the stag used in heraldry and the image on millions of Scottish shortbread tins. With its branching antlers and a mane of thick winter neck fur, it's colonised many places in the UK, including the Scottish Highlands, the Lake District, the forests of Thetford and Hampshire and the western moors.

Most mammals mate in spring, motivated to breed by warmer weather, but red deer are like sheep, driven by daylight length, not temperature. As the light changes and the days grow shorter, testosterone starts pumping in the stags ready for the rut and the females, or hinds, begin to ovulate. I've been told by experienced countrymen on Exmoor that during the season a really big stag can lose half its body weight chasing off other contenders, fighting its rivals in mortal antler-to-antler combat and finally mating with anything up to thirty females. The air echoes to the sound of their haunting moaning bellow during the autumn months. I can't describe it better than the naturalist and TV presenter Chris Packham, who said it sounds like a cross between a cow mooing and a wolf howling. The noise of the red stag at rut is certainly impressive, as he tries to exert his dominance over the other males in a macho contest for the right to mate with a harem of fertile females.

Wherever red deer live, you'll find a tradition of bolving competitions. It's the ideal contest for people with deep lungs and strong vocal cords because the aim is to gather on moorland at dusk and mimic the call of the red stag. It sounds utterly bananas, but it's taken seriously by experienced bolvers, with points awarded for volume and accuracy, plus the ultimate accolade – a red stag out in the gloom responding by bolving back. Champion bolvers say the secret of their success is plenty of practice, although I had to laugh when I heard about one prize-winner's rehearsals. Andy Batty from the Peak District admitted: 'I think the neighbours thought someone's being murdered these last few days.' One or two officially organised bolving contests have lapsed in recent years while some critics say bolving is unkind to the stags, so it will be interesting to see what the future holds for this annual spectacle.

A deer you might see more often if you live in the east or south of England – although they have also made their way to Wales and to parts of the north – is the muntjac deer. The racket they make as they mark their territory is unforgettable; they have a raspy, drawn-out bark that I think is horrendous! But they're an interesting and unusual mammal to spot in the fading light of an autumn evening: they look quite dog-like, with a hump back, a short tail and a pointed face. They were imported here from China by the Zoological Society of London as long ago as the 1830s, but today's wild herds are all down to the eleventh Duke of Bedford. The duke was fanatical about deer and in 1893 he introduced muntjac to his impressive deer collection at Woburn. Shortly afterwards some were released into the Bedfordshire woods nearby and along with muntjac which escaped a few years later, a feral population built up.

One of the Duke of Bedford's other favourites, and still the most common species in the UK, is the fallow deer. They're large, gingery-coloured animals with white spots and the bucks sport a pair of impressive palm-like antlers which they shed and re-grow every year. When they rut, the males have a loud, deep belching bark that comes straight from the belly.

The reason there are so many of them in the wild is down to the declining fortunes of the upper classes. After the First and Second World Wars, many old aristocratic families and the owners of Britain's great houses fell on hard times, and their country estates and parks tumbled into disarray. With no money to repair mile after mile of fences and walls, it wasn't long before the deer escaped and, left to their own devices, the population boomed. So while there are thousands of fallow deer in managed parkland today there are many more in wild grassland, commons and open woodland.

It's easy to assume that encouraging as big a population of wild animals as possible is the best thing for the environment, but that's not always the case. Fallow deer are a good example. Too many wild deer can have a detrimental effect on the ecology of an area, with hungry and often destructive animals damaging plantations, killing older trees by stripping off the bark, eating the understorey of younger trees and devouring cereal crops in the fields. I was amazed to discover that there are more deer running wild in the UK today than at any time in the last thousand years, with numbers increasing by at least 10 per cent year-on-year.

So what's the answer? Well, culling deer to keep the population under control and give some breathing space for other wildlife has always happened, with a healthy trade in deer meat. But the Covid pandemic caused enormous problems and two years of low culling followed. That's why the Wild Venison Project was launched to kick start a new trend for eating venison in restaurants, schools and hospitals. The not-for-profit movement was also set up to donate lean, sustainable venison to children and their families living in food poverty through a charity called the Country Food Trust. I became a patron of the Trust in 2020 and I know just what a difference it makes to the hungry and the homeless. Venison is low in fat and cholesterol, high in vitamins and minerals as well as being a very good wild natural source of protein. If you wanted to order some venison to have at home, I'd recommend using the Deer Box, a business run by the countryman and chef Mike Robinson, which supports the work of the Country Food Trust. Conservation and consumption can work in harmony, so you're doing your bit for nature not just by appreciating deer in their natural habitat but also when you buy venison for Sunday lunch or a special occasion.

Foraging

Every time I pick a blackberry from the brambles, the memories flood back of weekend blackberrying expeditions with my sisters when I was little. I'd nearly always end up with scratches on my arms and legs from the thorns and prickles, but all I cared about was the taste of the sweet fruit and a belly full of berries. Wild blackberries taste as good today and they're just one of the foods freely available to every one of us from Mother Nature's larder, providing a connection with our ancestors who relied on their seasonal bounty. I don't mind saying that my mum's blackberry and apple pie was the best. Custard, ice cream or cream? All three please!

While spring and summer blaze with the colours of heavy blossom and teeming flowers, the autumn palette is more subdued as the trees, shrubs and bushes give up their crop of fruit, berries, nuts and leaves. This is the hedgerow harvest, when the fare is every shade of red, purple, black and brown, which not only provides a nutritious, sustainable source of food, but also renews our link with nature and can boost mental and physical health. Who wouldn't want the reward of a basketful of freshly picked fruits and nuts after an afternoon outing in the autumn sunshine?

Picture	Where to find it	When to find it
blackberries	woods, heathland, parks and roadsides	September to October
rosehips	hedgerows, woodland edges and grassland	September to October and best picked after the first autumn frost
haws	hedgerows, woodland and scrub	March to November
sloes	woods, hedges, riverbanks and scrubland	September to November
beech nuts	woods or in copses on limestone, chalk and light loamy soil	September to November
crab apples	scrub, heathland, roadside verges and any well-drained soil	September to October

What it looks like	What the tree looks like	What you can do with it
dark fruits made up of a cluster of small juicy drupelets	a thicket of long prickly branches	jam, tarts, pies, crumble, chutney, sauce and cordial
bright red or orange apple-like fruit	dog rose is a scrambling shrub with sharp red thorns	rosehip syrup, tea, soup, sauce, jam, jelly and marmalade
small red berries like mini apples	a tangled bush with thorny branches	jam, jelly, chutney and country wine
a small dark purple or black plum covered in a pale 'bloom'	thorny tree or shrub with dark branches and white flowers	sloe gin (or vodka in our house because my wife doesn't like gin), wine, cider, jam and jelly
brown triangular nuts which fall inside a hard spiky husk	tall trees with a domed crown and smooth grey bark	roasted for eating, ground to make flour and crushed for oil
small hard fruit mostly coloured green and never bigger than a golf ball	a small tree with pinkish wood, gnarled branches and dark green oval leaves	crab apple liqueur, jelly and toffee apples

8

Walking in Autumn: Marks on the Land

One of the stories the landscape tells us is that we've been here for thousands of years, and walking through a field or hiking across the moors is simply following in the footprints of our forebears. That was brought home to me a few years ago when I discovered a Roman coin right outside the farmhouse. I'd opened the back door and spotted something next to the boot-scraper. I thought it might be a one pence coin, and knowing the old proverb 'see a penny, pick it up, and all day long you'll have good luck', I bent down to retrieve it. That's when I realised it wasn't a penny at all. This little remnant of everyday life had been in the soil for nearly two thousand years and, by chance, today was the day it got stuck to the bottom of my wellies and unwittingly brought back to the house. It's not legally treasure but it is incredibly precious to me.

Of course, you don't have to stumble across an

ancient object to see the past in the countryside. Here are the marks on the landscape you can find any time of year but ones I think look especially beautiful on a golden-tinged autumn walk.

Long barrows

At some time or another, we've all stopped to admire a lovely country view and seen an unusual earthen mound in the distance; a long grass-covered rectangle or a large, rounded hump that's obviously not a natural feature of the landscape. A quick check on a map shows it marked as Tumulus but if you get close up there's rarely a sign or an information board to explain what that means. What you'd be looking at is a 'house of the dead'. These huge manmade formations are called long barrows (or round barrows if they are hill-shaped) and they are where Neolithic tribes housed their dead relatives. The communal tombs were built around six thousand years ago, some with timber burial chambers and others with stone walls, and the sites were visited for regular rituals and ceremonies. This was an age when people believed that honouring the departed meant the spirit of their ancestors would look after the well-being of the living. Long barrows are the work of the first farmers who worked the land for crops and herded wild animals for meat, and there are hundreds of these Neolithic structures all over the country from Aberdeenshire in the north to the Sussex downlands in the south. The word barrow is an old dialect word for an earth mound, but they have other names around the UK; *howe* in the north of England, *low* in Cheshire and Staffordshire, while in Gloucestershire they're called *tumps*. We have a round barrow on the farm, thought to date from the time of a tribal chieftain known as Bem, which is where the name Bemborough originates. It's quite extraordinary to walk around the farm and see evidence that people have lived here and tilled the land for thousands of years, and sobering to think that my turn caring for these precious acres is a tiny fraction of that time. It reminds me to do my best to leave it in a better state than when I found it, for the benefit of the next generation.

Once you've got an eye for spotting long barrows, you'll start noticing them on hilltops, in vales and even in places you've known for years but never recognised as historic landscapes. I think long barrows are remarkable reminders of the people in our past, and an everlasting monument to the Ancients.

Iron Age hill forts

Iron Age hill forts came later than long barrows but there are many more of them, well over three thousand across the UK, and they are visible today as earthworks, dents and banks, or a series of contours on the summit of our most prominent hills. Although they're called forts, they weren't all military bases; the phrase is used to mean a defended enclosed community, so that includes meeting places, homesteads and summer pasture for sheep and cattle. The dents are all that's left of the ditches, and the banks are the remains of the ramparts. Imagine what a massive task it would have been to construct a hill fort using primitive tools – picks made of deer antler, spades made of wood and wicker baskets to remove the spoil.

One of the most unusual hill forts in Britain is just a few miles from where I live: Salmonsbury camp is on the outskirts of the tourist village of Bourton-on-the-Water and it's a hill fort that's not on a hill. In fact, it sits in low land between two meandering rivers with nearby water meadows in what is now a nature reserve. The land has been farmed for six thousand years and today it is grazed by an organic herd of rare breed Old Gloucester cattle. So what was going on? Well, Salmonsbury is from the later Iron Age, about 100 BC, when life was more hospitable and there was no need to build defences to repel raiders. Instead, it was probably a centre for markets, trade and tribal gatherings, attracting people from the surrounding countryside to meet up and exchange handcrafted goods and livestock. The site was abandoned a few hundred years later during the Roman occupation, but a gravel knoll above the river with the eroded traces of a bank and a ditch are reminders of a bustling past.

Ridge and furrow

Late in the afternoon, when the sun is low in the sky and shadows grow long, the ancient ways of farming the land become visible. Gentle undulations in the open fields, like the ripples of a wave, become easier to see in the filtered light an hour or two before dusk. These are scars in the soil left behind by the plough in the Middle Ages, pulled by a team of oxen going back and forth, year after year, generation after generation. These traces of the past are called ridge and furrow. Peasant labourers would work the fields of the local squire or the lord of the manor, but they were allowed to grow their own crops too, on communal land which they shared with other villagers. The parcels of land were divided up into narrow strips, with each strip tended by a different tenant, in an open-field system (open because there were no hedgerows, walls or boundary fences). The ridges were caused by the plough blade throwing soil up into an elongated mound and the resulting furrows became an excellent method of drainage with water trickling down the troughs into ditches at the foot of the field, where even today you can see reeds growing. Look out for curved troughs and 'S'-shaped ridges, caused by large teams of oxen turning at either end of the furrow and bringing the plough back round for the return journey. No such thing as a reversible plough in the Middle Ages!

Ridge and furrow can be seen everywhere, including right outside my house in what we call the home paddock, but the finest examples are in the English Midlands and East Anglia, in fields which were returned to grassland, pasture or sheep grazing and have never seen a modern plough. I often spot the tell-tale corrugated effect on the land if I'm driving out through the lanes of Oxfordshire, Warwickshire or the Vale of Evesham in winter, when a dusting of snow is enough to reveal those faint, ancient creases. Marks of the past, cut and turned by boys whose names we will never know, but whose labour is evident to us centuries on. Wonderfully, there are two villages where the medieval open strip system is still practised. At Braunton in Devon, the Great Field has been farmed this way since the 1200s, while at Laxton in Nottinghamshire the fields are inspected by a local 'jury' every November in an age-old tradition to ensure no one has ploughed their neighbour's strip.

The ridge and furrow method left us another legacy. Our traditional system of British weights and measures owes a debt of gratitude to the medieval ploughboys and the stick they used to control their oxen. It was called a rod, a pole or a perch (depending on where they lived) and at five-and-a-half yards long, it was the perfect length to reach the farthest ox. Laid four times across a field, it measured twenty-two yards, and forty times down a field made 220 yards; that area is one acre. Meanwhile bells should be ringing if you're a sports fan, because twenty-two yards is the length of a cricket pitch and 220 yards is one furrow long, or furlong, which is the standard way of measuring horse races.

Pillow mounds

I wonder how many people realise that rabbits aren't a native British species? They are originally from southern Europe and archaeologists know the Romans brought some here as part of a menagerie of 'exotic pets'. But it wasn't until William the Conqueror and his army invaded in 1066 that the fur-covered, long-eared mammals were introduced in large numbers to run wild across the countryside. To help rabbits adapt to their new colder surroundings the Normans built artificial warrens where the animals could live safely and breed. It was a great example of medieval animal husbandry and meant that for the first time rabbits could be properly farmed for their meat and fur.

Today around two thousand of these old warren sites are still visible across southern England and Wales, although most people have no idea what they are.

From Hatfield Forest in Essex to Mynydd Melyn in Pembrokeshire there are huge cigar-shaped grassy mounds on hillsides, in parkland and beneath the spreading branches of horse chestnut trees. These shallow formations in the ground give the impression of large pillows made of earth which is why they're called pillow mounds. In the Middle Ages rabbits were known as coneys and the pillow mounds were called coney garths, meaning an enclosure for rabbits. Pick up a map and you'll find dozens of locations where the rabbit farming of the past lives on in the place names of the present: there's Coneyhurst in Sussex, Coney Hill in Gloucester and Coneygar Hill in Dorset. There's even a field called Coneys on our farm and I'm sure there are other farmers and landowners all over the country who could say something similar.

Ha-has

Despite the funny name, there was a serious reason behind the building of these important landscape features. The aristocracy and wealthy landowners in the 1700s didn't want the beautiful views from their country houses ruined by walls and fences. So a new way was needed to keep roaming livestock away from the manicured lawns and out of the formal gardens. Instead of putting a barrier *up*, they dug a deep ditch *down* to create a large step supported by a brick or stone wall on the inner side, all the way to the level of the surrounding turf at the top. The result looked a little bit like a one-sided moat, but from the windows of the grand house it created the illusion of a flat, open vista. Before machines, these huge lawns were cut using horse drawn mowers. To avoid heavy horses like the Suffolk Punch leaving unsightly footprints in the grass, they wore large leather boots over their hooves to spread the weight. The ha-has of England are well loved and looked after in the twenty-first century and you can see them for yourself at Berrington Hall in Herefordshire, Petworth House in Sussex and the gardens at Kedleston in Derbyshire, among many others.

Chalk figures

Bold, over-sized and mysterious, white chalk figures stand out brazenly in various places across the soft green baize of the south and west. The most famous and enigmatic chalk figure is the Uffington White Horse which sits on the scarp of the Berkshire Downs beside the ancient Ridgeway, which follows the hilltops all the way from Wiltshire to Buckinghamshire. But it's not from the prehistoric trackway that I usually see this distinctive landmark, it's from the snatched glimpses I get of it through the trees when I drive between Oxford and Swindon. It's a distant view, but then it always seems to be a distant view because if you stand on the hill itself you can't see the whole horse. Its sheer size means that close up it's just a series of random chalk-filled trenches which make no sense on the sloping uneven ground. And, of course, it's not a complete figure, it's more a disjointed suggestion of a horse made up of stylised long white curves and lines; two of the legs aren't attached to the body, the head is a box and there's a dot for an eye. If I make it sound like a 1930s surrealist painting, that's exactly the impression it gives!

Uffington isn't just the most distinctive chalk figure in the country, it's also the oldest. Recent excavations have confirmed it was created at least three thousand years ago and it's been a source of fascination ever since (as long ago as the Middle Ages it was being described as 'one of the wonders of the ancient world'). No one can say for certain why the Uffington White Horse is there, but at about the same time it was created, late Bronze Age farmers were marking out their territory in the landscape, establishing what we would call estates today, and it's thought the carving might have been set up on such a prominent hillside as an impressive badge. As if the locals were saying 'This is us – we are here' and literally shouting it from the hills.

Uffington was certainly the inspiration for many of the white horses which followed. Among the most photographed are the ones at Westbury, Cherhill and Pewsey in Wiltshire, the county which can claim to be the carved horse capital of England with more chalky equines galloping over its hills down the centuries than any other part of the country. There are other figures, including The Long Man of Wilmington in Sussex (the guardian of the South Downs famously holding two 'staves' or poles); a crown at Wye in Kent (the idea of agricultural students who wanted to mark Edward VII's coronation in 1902) and a kiwi on Salisbury Plain (created by New Zealand troops waiting to be demobilised after the First World War in 1919).

There is one piece of hill art which mustn't be left out. Known to millions as the 'Rude Man', and officially called the Cerne Abbas Giant, he's been causing sniggers in Dorset since Saxon times. The figure is a club-wielding man who is obviously naked, or as Historic England bashfully calls him 'bold and anatomically impressive'! For obvious reasons it's been suggested that he was originally a fertility symbol, or a depiction of a long-forgotten god, but he's certainly good news for local tourism.

What's tantalising about every one of the chalk figures is that left alone, they would all disappear. The weather would dull and dirty the chalk, grass and weeds would eventually grow over them and within a generation they would be gone. It has happened to dozens of historic hill carvings already, lost to nature forever. So to preserve the ones we have left, they're cleaned and re-chalked regularly to keep them gleaming white in a tradition called 'scouring'. Every time it happens, dozens of volunteers empty their garden sheds of spades, pick-axes and brooms, and head off to the hills where a great deal of chalk is used to bring the figures back to their best. When the Whipsnade White Lion was given a facelift in 2017, it took six months and fifty lorry-loads of chalk to resurface the figure.

But today's willing workforce is tiny compared to the numbers who turned up when the Uffington White Horse was scoured in the mid-1800s. Over the years people from the towns and villages in the wide expanse of vale below the hills had wanted to do their bit to restore the local landmark, and to celebrate their good deed afterwards, of course. These post-work revels became increasingly popular, with sporting contests and food and drink on offer. Handbills for the events described them as 'games, gaiety and gore'. In September 1857, organisers really went overboard, advertising wrestling, cheese-rolling, backswords (a type of sword fighting), greasy-pole climbing, donkey racing and the promise that 'a pig will be turned out on the down, to be the prize of the man who catches him'. The result was pandemonium. Thirty thousand people descended on White Horse Hill, obviously tempted less by the idea of a day's hard work – and more by the prospect of winning a pig!

The village church

Churches serve a very practical purpose for wanderers, hikers and ramblers. The towers and spires have always been excellent navigation aids, even for stragglers without a map, and it's especially true in the flattest landscapes such as the Somerset Levels, the Vale of York and the famously low-lying Fens of Cambridgeshire and Lincolnshire.

As well as being the most obvious local landmark, the church is usually the oldest building in a parish and many have been standing for a thousand years. In Essex there's an abundance of church buildings and remains which are much older and go back as far as the seventh and eighth centuries, such as St Peter-on-the-Wall at Bradwell, St Mary's at Prittlewell, St Helen's Chapel at Colchester and, extraordinarily, the oldest wooden church in the world at Greensted near Chipping Ongar which dates back to 845 AD.

Wherever you live, there will be history to be gleaned by looking at your parish church. When Saxon and Norman churches were constructed, the best building materials were often the ones closest to hand, so we see honey-coloured limestone in the Cotswolds, flint in East Anglia and granite in Aberdeenshire. It seems as if the churches, and the cottages nearby, are part of the surrounding landscape, giving the impression that they've risen straight out of the ground.

Dating a church just by looking at its shape and style isn't straightforward; down the centuries, important buildings have always been remodelled to suit the tastes and trends of the day. But when you come across a church on a country walk, there are some architectural clues to help work out its age:

Saxon	600–1066	semi-circular door and window arches herringbone stonework tall slim doorways
Norman	1066–1200	semi-circular arches vaulted ceilings large round pillars
perpendicular	1350–1550	spires replaced with towers impressive large stained-glass windows columns crowned with carvings from nature, the military or the monarchy

If you love churches, for whatever reason, you might want to look into the work done by a group of like-minded enthusiasts who strive to keep these impressive and surprising buildings in good repair and open to the public. The Historic Churches Trust has helped safeguard thousands of churches and chapels over recent years thanks, in part, to support from some well-known names including actor and adventurer Sir Michael Palin, travel writer Bill Bryson and BBC news presenter Huw Edwards.

Autumn vs fall

We all know what autumn looks like – increasingly bare trees, frosty mornings, a smoky dampness in the air. But how did the period between summer and winter get its name, and what's it called in other countries?

Do you ever roll your eyes when people (who really should know better) refer to autumn as 'fall'? Of course our great British reserve means we'll just smile and say nothing, but we all know in our hearts that autumn is the correct English language word and fall is just a modern Americanism. Except that's not strictly true – in fact, both terms started right here in Blighty.

Until the fourteenth century autumn was known simply as harvest, and as most of the population was involved in farming it seemed natural that the task dominating their lives also described the time of year. At some point in the 1300s it started being called autumn, a word derived from the Latin autumnus, although no one quite knows its origins (it might be linked to the ancient Egyptian deity, Autun, god of the setting sun). Then in the 1500s, a more romantic, descriptive phrase took off – 'the fall of the leaves' – and before long it was abbreviated to 'the fall'.

In the 1600s when British settlers were establishing colonies in North America, the English language went with them, including the words autumn and fall. Within a couple of hundred years the Brits had decided on autumn, while the New World preferred fall. And we've never agreed on it since!

Here's what autumn is known as in a few other languages:

French: *l'automne*
German: *Herbst*
Italian: *autunno*
Spanish: *otoño*
Swahili: *vuli*
Turkish: *sonbahar*

9

Michaelmas

Autumn was the 'season of mists and mellow fruitfulness' in the mind of the Romantic poet John Keats, but to me and for thousands of other people all over the British Isles it means something entirely different – the start of the farming year. Once the harvest has been safely gathered in and the evidence of the previous twelve months' hard graft is sitting in the grain stores, all thoughts can turn to the coming year. The fields are ploughed, winter wheat, barley and oilseed rape are sown and straw is baled up, ready as bedding and feed for the animals in the long, cold months ahead.

But traditionally it wasn't just the crop cycle that dictated the start of the agricultural year. It was usual for farm tenancies to be renewed in the autumn, normally at Michaelmas on 29 September. Would the hard-working farmer and his family stay, or would they prepare for the upheaval and uncertainty of a new farm, a new home and a new landlord? In many cases, it wasn't their choice to make. For more fortunate farmers, the end of tenancies in the autumn was a convenient moment because they could take their newly harvested crops with them, while the incoming tenant could start from scratch and plant new crops out in the fields.

It was also the time for taking on new servants and labourers, and in market towns all over the country hiring fairs took place where everyone fit for service and needing work would turn up, trying to catch the eye of prospective employers. Long before CVs and LinkedIn, these workless hopefuls brought symbols of their trade to the fair as a recruitment device – shepherds might wear a piece of wool in their hats or carry crooks, carters would display some whipcord, thatchers put woven straw in their lapels and, famously, housemaids would bring a broom or mop. That's where the term 'Mop Fair' originated. Even though it's been almost a hundred years since the last servants and farm hands were hired this way, the funfairs and markets which pop up in city centres and town squares the length and breadth of the UK every autumn are still called 'Mops'.

There were also big Michaelmas horse fairs and sheep sales, and the traditional time for shepherds to put the ram to the ewes was when they got back from Michaelmas Fair. The financial year started at Michaelmas, the local courts, or Quarter Sessions, met, and the first school term of the academic year was named after it. Michaelmas was a day that mattered a great deal to our ancestors and I think some of their feasts and festivities are well worth restoring (and an excuse for a bit of a knees-up!).

Another name for 29 September was Goose Day, because it was customary to eat roast goose to celebrate the feast of St Michael (which is how Michaelmas gets its name – Michael's Mass). Historically, the goose played a vital role in the relationship between the farm tenant and the local squire or land-owner. Quarterly rents were due on Michaelmas Day and along with the payment, farm workers were advised to give a gift of a juicy goose to their landlord to curry favour for the months to come. Really canny tenants would have raised enough geese not to miss one, leaving them with a few birds to sell and make enough cash to pay the bills. And if the cottagers feasted on one of their own geese as well, superstition was on their side:

Eat a goose on Michaelmas Day,
Want not for money all the year.

There are different types of eating goose, but the very best birds are 'green' geese – young birds, usually less than four months old, which are too small to stuff so are boiled or roasted and served with a sharp sauce. Fed on grass and the stubble left in the fields after the

185

wheat harvest, they are leaner than the Christmas goose which develops more fat with the cold weather. 'Green' geese are at their absolute prime in autumn, and even if your local butcher doesn't usually stock goose, they will almost certainly supply one for your Michaelmas celebration if you ask early enough.

Once you've finished carving the Michaelmas goose, the question is 'What do I do with the wishbone?' You might think two guests pulling the wishbone is a Christmas tradition when the turkey's on the table, but they're recreating what our farming forebears did on 29 September with the goose wishbone. For our ancestors, the apprehension wasn't over after closing their eyes and making a wish. It was said that if the cooked bones came out brown the winter ahead would be mild, but white bones meant months of snow and ice.

If you don't want to stay in to celebrate, you could go to a Goose Fair instead. The Nottingham Goose Fair draws huge crowds who are attracted by the travelling funfair, the neon lights and the loud music – but it started as a livestock auction in the Middle Ages to provide birds in time for Michaelmas. Remarkably in the last 750 years (or thereabouts) the Goose Fair has been cancelled only a handful of times: in 1646 because of bubonic plague, during the two World Wars and more recently due to coronavirus restrictions.

There's also the Tavistock Goosey Fair in Devon

which dates back to the twelfth century and is still a big deal today, with stalls, stands and entertainment taking over the town centre streets, the Showmen's Guild of Great Britain out in force and livestock sales at the local cattle market. On the opposite side of Devon, the village of Colyford revived its Goose Fayre in 1980 and has kept it going with gusto ever since. I take my hat off to this small community which works hard to recreate the atmosphere of the traditional Michaelmas celebration. The locals parade through the village in medieval costume, there are strolling players, archery competitions and even a greasy pole climbing contest.

Another old Michaelmas tradition is the annual Urswick rush-bearing ceremony in Lancashire. It started in the days when homes and churches had earthen floors which had to be covered with rushes for warmth, and the custom of taking stems and flowers to church gradually evolved into a religious ceremony. Every Michaelmas Day there's marching, banners, a brass band as well as a Rush Queen, then after the service it's back to the local school for tea and ginger-bread. Who could refuse?

Not everything associated with Michaelmas was quite so popular with vicars. You probably won't be thanked for reviving a noisy and thoroughly mischievous custom called Crack-Nut Sunday. At Kingston in Surrey, the congregation would take nuts into church on the Sunday before St Michael's Day and bring the service to a grinding halt by cracking the shells and drowning out the minister's sermon. It sounds like chaos. No one's quite sure why nuts were associated with Michaelmas (apart from the fact that there are plenty of them around in September), although as far back as the 1700s the novelist and poet Oliver Goldsmith wrote about parishioners in Wakefield who 'religiously cracked nuts on Michaelmas'.

A final footnote to all the talk of September nuts, geese and Mop Fairs: look out for the Michaelmas daisy. It's a welcome dash of colour late in the season, a little like the big mauve sister of the common daisy. It's a garden flower which brightens up borders with its yellow centres and long blue or purple petals but nature being what it is, it's now found growing wild on canal banks, railway embankments and on marshy grassland. A well-established field of wild Michaelmas daisies will catch the eye, looking like heather from a distance, and I love seeing them.

September, with its surprisingly sun-blessed days, seems to amble into October. By contrast November definitely makes its presence felt; altogether colder, crisper and damper. It's when you're most likely to see what some old dairymen call 'half cow fog' – the thick morning mist which sits at ground level, shrouding the legs of grazing cattle in a grey murk.

The brisk westerly wind and the early dusk are telling us that the transition from autumn to winter is underway and that it's time to button up for the hardest season of all.

The Farmer's Diary

Here's what you can expect to see from farmers during autumn:

	Arable farming	Livestock farming
September	Cultivating is the most visible activity on the land. Winter barley and winter wheat are drilled (planted). Potatoes are harvested, orchard fruit peaks with apples, pears and plums, while blackberries and the last crop of raspberries are picked on soft fruit farms.	Autumn calving in dairy herds. This year's lambs continue to be selected for market. Breeding ewe and ram sales are taking place at livestock auctions all over the country.
October	In the Midlands and east of England the sugar beet harvest starts. It's also pumpkin season, of course! Hedge-cutting begins once birds have abandoned their nests.	It's tupping time as the ram meets the ewes in mating season. Cattle on summer pasture are brought in for the winter.
November	Corn sales. Harvesting of Christmas trees is underway, a useful diversification on many farms.	Pregnant ewes are scanned to determine how many lambs we can expect in the New Year.

Five other things to see or do in autumn

1. Go to Westonbirt

In my opinion the best place to see autumn colour in the UK is Westonbirt Arboretum in Gloucestershire. The tree collection was started there in 1829 and developed with relish by an enterprising character called Robert Holford, a wealthy landowner and politician who was said to have been the richest commoner in England. It's not just any old woodland, it's one of the most important plant collections in the world with 2,500 different species, fifteen thousand individual specimens, 140 of the tallest trees in the British Isles and some of the rarest trees on the entire planet. Among all of that are the national collections of walnut, lime, bladdernut, maple and Japanese maple cultivars. So think of it as the British Museum of trees!

It's a great place for a day out at any time of the year, but Westonbirt comes into its own in autumn. 'A riot of colour' is the season's most over-used phrase, but at the height of autumn that's exactly what's on show at the National Arboretum. It's a seasonal highlight that's been enjoyed by generations, but a completely new way of seeing the kaleidoscope of autumn was introduced in 2016 when a treetop walkway opened at Westonbirt, giving magnificent views from high up in the canopy.

2. Celebrate Nutcrack night

Not to be confused with Crack-nut Sunday (page 187), Nutcrack night is a very old custom from the north of England, Scotland and Ireland which took place every year on 31 October, All Hallows' Evening (nearly always shortened to Hallowe'en). But this had nothing to do with ghosts, ghouls or witches on broomsticks; instead, it was about flames and fortune-telling. Lighting ceremonial fires the night before All Hallows' Day was usual in many parts of the country as relief for the souls of lost loved ones suffering in purgatory, and that fiery theme was carried over to Nutcrack night. Cold October nights meant families gathering round fires for warmth while they ate autumn-gathered apples, berries and nuts. When the hazelnuts, chestnuts and beech mast started being thrown into the flames for fun, superstitions grew about the burning shells. A young man wanting to know who to marry would name two nuts after his sweethearts and throw them both in the fire. The one which burned the brightest was the lover he should choose. There was a similar tradition for anyone wanting to know what the future held for their marriage. Again two nuts went into the fire. If they burned brightly side by side, the relationship would be sweetness and light. But if they hissed, leapt or crackled in the heat, it was a prediction of bad temper, strife or even separation. If you're not keen on scary fancy dress and trick-or-treating, you could always revive Nutcrack night next Hallowe'en – if you dare risk a row with your loved one!

3. See a murmuration of starlings

'Murmurate' is a word that's wonderful to say, and describes a natural phenomenon that's even more wonderful to see. It's been called 'the ballet of the skies' and it happens in autumn and winter when starlings roost together, packed tightly in huge communal flocks. The magic occurs just before dusk when hundreds, thousands or, if you're lucky, anything up to a million starlings take to the wing in a breath-taking aerial display, swirling and twisting in a fast-moving swarm. Despite flying at speeds of 90mph the birds are perfectly synchronised and never collide as the great dark mass curls and contorts in the air. How do they do it? It seems that individual starlings in the air communicate with the five or six birds nearest to them only. They copy their neighbours' manoeuvres and when that's multiplied thousands of times the result is the 'waves' which ripple through the flock as they spiral in the sky. I never get tired of seeing the starlings do their aerial acrobatics above the large laurel hedge next to my house, and I'm usually alerted by the whooshing sound and the beat of their wings.

What's remarkable, when you consider that we sent men to the moon more than half a century ago, is that scientists are still baffled about the reason for starling murmurations. One theory is that it's a way of warding off predators such as buzzards and sparrowhawks, with the old rule at play that there's safety in numbers. Birds of prey focus on a single target so will never attack an entire flock with their talons out hoping for the best. The other idea is that flying en masse is a signal to other starlings to gather for the roost. It's warmer for a single starling to spend a cold winter's night within a large flock, sharing the body heat of the other birds, so is the sky-dance a sign that it's time for bed?

There are no guarantees when a murmuration will

take place or where, and while some displays last for half an hour or more, some will be over in a few minutes. But when the birds return to their roosts the scene is as dramatic as the murmuration itself: without warning the entire flock will suddenly funnel towards the trees as if they've been sucked into a vacuum, and in seconds they've gone completely with the frenetic jaw-dropping spectacle replaced by an eerie stillness.

If you've never witnessed a murmuration then you must put it at the top of your bucket list. Probably the best place in the country to experience this starling spectacular is Ham Wall in Somerset. It's one of the nature reserves created from abandoned peat workings in the Avalon Marshes not far from Glastonbury. It's so good, and popular, that they've even got a Starling Hotline to help spectators find the best vantage point.

4. Eat the season's fruit

I'm a big fan of seasonal eating; British Brussels sprouts in winter, Evesham asparagus in spring and English strawberries in summer. They're fresher than year-round foods, they don't travel as far to get to the shelves and they definitely taste better ... plus it's great news for British farmers and growers. Autumn for me is summed up by images of colourful baskets of ripe, juicy fruit just brought in from the fields and orchards.

We think of plums – the colourful fleshy oval-shaped fruit with the sweet-tart taste – as a summer fruit but, in fact, they ripen, one variety after the other, for four months right through to October. Three different types of plum are grown in the UK: dessert plums for eating such as Cambridge Gage and Jefferson; culinary plums for cooking (they make delicious, juicy jam) which include Czar and Marjorie's Seedling; and dual-purpose ones which will do both jobs handsomely, like Avalon and Oullins Golden Gage. But the variety everyone has heard of is the Victoria. It is to plums what Conference is to pears – the most widely grown and popular plum in the UK, and it's been the nation's favourite for well over a hundred years.

One of the unsung heroes of the autumn is the perry pear. These are as varied as any other seasonal fruit, although they tend to be rounder than a teardrop-shaped Conference, and like cider apples you can't treat them as an eater. They're purely for juicing, fermenting and turning into that delicious drink of the country, perry. It's widely believed that perry pears will only grow well in sight of May Hill, the prominent wooded sandstone dome that rises up between Gloucester and Ross-on-Wye. Sure enough, the hill's nearest neighbours in the three counties of Gloucestershire, Herefordshire and Worcestershire are the best perry pear growers in the land. There are hotly contested competitions for the best perry at the Royal Three Counties Show in Malvern every June, and if you find yourself in the bar sharing a bottle or two with the local perry aficionados, a word of warning. Don't call it pear cider. Sacrilege!

There's one fruit which I think should be much better known – quince. It makes sensational jelly as well as jam and marmalade. The fruit looks like a bright yellow pear with a powdery citrus aroma that's a bit like a cross between the smell of an apple and a pear. In fact, in ancient times they were called 'golden apples'. If you can find a quince tree, and they're not particularly common, it will be in season from October to December with the hard, tart fruit impossible to miss. You can't eat them from the tree, but once they're made into a lovely rose-coloured jelly and served on a cheese board or with a plate of roast pork or game, they're sweet and tasty. If you're unfamiliar with quince but the name rings a bell, you're probably half-remembering a bedtime story from your childhood. It pops up in Edward Lear's timeless nonsense poem 'The Owl and the Pussy-Cat':

> *They dined on mince and slices of quince,*
> *Which they ate with a runcible spoon;*
> *And hand in hand, on the edge of the sand,*
> *They danced by the light of the moon . . .*

5. Spot the Harvest Moon and the Hunter's Moon

We've been moon-gazing forever and the sight of a full moon has always been a thing of wonder and mystery. 'A full moon means good weather' is a popular saying that's lasted. 'It'll be a wet month when there are two full moons in it' is another. The traditional names we've given to full moons are pretty wonderful too: the Wolf Moon in January, the Growing Moon in April, the Corn Moon in August. In autumn there are two to keep an eye on: the Harvest Moon in September or October and the Hunter's Moon in October or November.

The Harvest Moon is the one nearest the autumn equinox (when the length of daylight and night-time are equal) and it will always appear bigger than usual because it's nearer the horizon, so the moon isn't just very bright in the sky, it also rises early. When most lives were dictated by work on the land, having a big bright moon giving valuable light at this time of year extended the time farm workers could labour in the fields gathering in the crops. I think just about everyone's heard of the Harvest Moon, even people who have nothing to do with farming or astronomy. Thanks to a very old song called 'Shine on Harvest Moon' and the singer/songwriter Neil Young's bestselling 1990s album and single 'Harvest Moon', it's found its way into everyday language.

The Hunter's Moon is similar, with the tilt of the earth on its axis meaning the moon hangs lower in the sky and – because we see it through a thicker atmosphere which scatters short-wavelength blue light – it has a red or orange tinge. For our ancient ancestors, with no calendars or clocks, lunar activity was crucial to help them track time and the Hunter's Moon is mentioned as far back as the Anglo Saxons, more than 1,500 years ago. The huge red moon sent the message that winter was on its way and the time had come for hunting wild animals before the harshest weather arrived – so the Hunter's Moon it became.

WINTER

Chill December brings the sleet,
Blazing fire, and Christmas treat.
January brings the snow,
makes our feet and fingers glow.

February brings the rain,
Thaws the frozen lake again.

From 'The Months' by Sara Coleridge

Introduction

The winter might be tough, especially on isolated farms and in lonely locations, but there is something exhilarating about a blast of cold air on your face or the crunch of frost under your boots first thing in the morning. Like everyone, I've got a few stories of wintery weather and close shaves in the snow. Slithering through the ice to get frozen pipes working out in the fields, or knee-deep in snow to get extra hay to the animals, and years after it was shown on *Countryfile*, people still ask me about the time I was caught in a sudden blizzard. I was helping my old friend Neil Heseltine move his herd of Belted Galloway cattle in the Yorkshire Dales when the weather took a sudden change for the worse. We were blinded by swirling snow and the drifts were so deep against a five-bar gate I had to start digging away with my hands to get it open. 'Give me the sunny Cotswolds, any day,' I said for the whole world to hear.

The cattle didn't bat an eyelid of course. Heads down, they trudged on regardless, wondering what all the fuss was about. And that's what I remember most about that day – the hardy, no-nonsense live-stock. Breeds like these have always been part of my life and they're one of the reasons I get up in the morning; even when the wind howls and there's ice at the window. There's nothing boring about the winter, I can tell you, especially when the weather really gets the blood pumping.

Sara Coleridge's poem 'The Months', written in the nineteenth century, follows the year with lovely brisk descriptions of each month and, naturally, it starts with January and ends in December. But I think re-arranging it to run from March to February – as I've done in this book, to illustrate the seasons – brings a wonderful sense of hope to the ending: 'February brings the rain/Thaws the frozen lake *again*.' We're so lucky in the British Isles to have the seasons we do; even on the darkest nights, or on the coldest, most difficult days out on the farm, we know warmer times are just around the corner.

10

Long Nights

One of the obvious changes that winter brings is shorter days. Most of us wake to darkness, and return home from a day's work after sundown. If we are lucky enough to see any sunshine during the day, it's weak and casts long shadows on the ground, like a lamp with the dimmer switch turned on. But instead of railing against it, I think it's better to lean into the winter darkness and enjoy the opportunities it brings.

At the beginning of this book, I recommended getting up early, wrapping up in warm clothes, and sitting outside to enjoy the dawn chorus. Now we're in winter, it's time to wrap up warm and go outside again – but this time at night to enjoy the stars. One of the best things about living in the countryside is the comparative lack of light pollution from cities and towns. Sitting outside with a blanket for warmth on a crisp, clear night, flask in hand, and simply staring up at the twinkling heavens above is a calming and humbling thing to do.

Here in Gloucestershire there's a much-loved poem about dark skies, the shimmering heavens and bright moonlight. 'This Night the Stars' was written by Leonard Clark, a friend of the great John Betjeman, and he compares the stellar display to precious stones glinting over Birdlip Hill, a famous spur of the Cotswold escarpment. The poem goes on to paint a beautiful picture of fields lit by moon beams and the lanterns and streetlamps in town glistening like the stars above them. It doesn't mention winter by name but when I hear it read aloud or sung to music, I always imagine that Clark was staring up at a night sky in December.

You certainly don't need to be an astronomy aficionado like Brian Cox or Dara Ó Briain to star spot; you can enjoy the night sky for what it is and while I can't pretend to know all the constellations off by heart, being able to spot a couple makes staring up at the stars all the more exciting. There are two particular stars that are a practical introduction to the art of stargazing for beginners. The first is the most famous, at least to those of us who live in the northern hemisphere: the North Star, which is (relatively) easy to find in Britain because it sits in pretty much the same position in the sky throughout the night, not rising or setting like many others. Proper astronomers call it Polaris, or the pole star, and it's a great beacon for people lost in the dark because it points the way true north (that's geographical north, rather than magnetic north which is the slightly different direction a compass points). Because the North Star is located above the earth's rotational axis, it appears to stand still while the other stars seem to spin slowly around it. Interestingly the southern hemisphere doesn't have an equivalent to the North Star. It's sheer luck that there is a star marking the Celestial North Pole – the Celestial South Pole doesn't have a star bright enough or close enough to be helpful to anyone looking for geographical south.

To find the North Star, you need to locate the Plough – also known as the Big Dipper. The Plough is part of a constellation called Ursa Major and you will almost certainly have noticed it before. It contains four bright stars arranged in a wonky rectangle, with another three bright stars making up the handle.

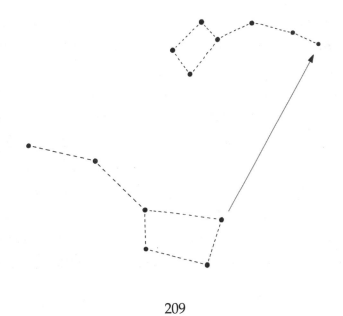

Personally, I think it looks like a saucepan and if you think about it that way, the star you want to be singling out to help find Polaris is on the top of the saucepan, furthest away from the handle. From this star you can draw an imaginary line to Polaris – it's one of the stars that makes up Ursa Minor, also known as the Little Dipper. The Little Dipper gets its nickname because it looks similar to the Big Dipper: it also has four bright stars in a rectangular shape, with another three making up a handle – it's just a smaller version. The last star in the Little Dipper's handle, the one the star in the Big Dipper is in line with, is Polaris, the North Star.

Whether you call it the Plough or the Big Dipper, those are just seven stars contained within Ursa Major, which is made up of more stars to form a bigger shape. I say shape; it's quite tricky to make head or tail of it! In fact, we *should* be looking for a head and a tail within it because it's supposed to represent a bear – Ursa Major in Latin means 'Great Bear' – and humans have watched it and wondered about it for millennia. By the second century AD it was included in an astrological treatise by the Greek mathematician and geographer Ptolemy. There are many myths and stories associated with the Great Bear and the Plough/ Big Dipper which sits within it. Perhaps the most British tale concerns the Plough. King Arthur was said to be living in the sky somewhere near Polaris, and so over time the Plough became known as King Arthur's chariot – so-called because he would use it to ride around the North Star.

However, the North Star isn't the shiniest star in the sky. That accolade belongs to Sirius, a name meaning 'glowing' or 'scorching' in the original Greek, and it's twice as visible as the next brightest: Canopus.

I've always known Sirius by its alternative name, the Dog Star, given to it because it's in the constellation of Canis Major, the big hunting dog. If you've heard the phrase 'the dog days of summer' to mean really hot, sultry weather, well that comes from Sirius. The Ancient Greeks and Romans thought that the heat was caused by the Dog Star rising in the sky alongside the sun, and the two combined brought punishing conditions, heatwaves, drought and fever. And if your kids are mad about Harry Potter, like mine were when they were little, it's easy to work out why the boy wizard's godfather, Sirius, turns into a big black dog.

You can find Sirius simply by looking for the brightest star in the sky, but to be certain you've found the right one, locate Orion's belt. Orion is a big constellation which is supposed to look like a hunter with a bow and arrow. His belt is the easiest part to spot, as it's made up of three stars quite close together which sit almost in a straight line. Those three stars are aligned with Sirius, which is separated from the belt, often closer to the horizon than Orion. Keep in

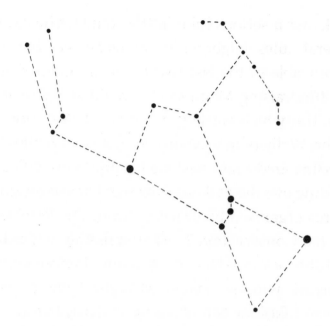

mind that Orion and Sirius appear to rise and set in the night sky so you won't always be able to see them, but evenings in January and February (in the northern hemisphere) are the best times to spot Sirius. The planets in our solar system can sometimes appear brighter than the stars, so if you're not sure if you're looking at a star or a planet, think of the nursery rhyme 'Twinkle, Twinkle Little Star'. Planets rarely twinkle (they only do in specific atmospheric conditions), whereas stars do.

Getting to know the stars and planets is one of the benefits of night walking. I don't mean an amble around the garden or a short stroll down the road after dark, but a serious hike in the countryside covering several miles. Night walking has become incredibly fashionable in the last two decades, popularised by the fundraising Moon Walks in aid of breast cancer charities which started in the late 1990s. While the Moon Walkers mostly stay in towns and cities, they have inspired a new pastime in rural areas with teams heading into the darkness together and official guided events organised by everyone from The Ramblers to the Bat Conservation Trust. Torches are left at home and the lack of artificial light from lampposts, neon signs and windows takes a bit of getting used to, but it doesn't take long before our natural night vision kicks in. When it's dark, the pupils at the front of our eyes become larger to allow more light in and the receptors which give us our vision switch from colour-sensitive cone cells to light-sensitive rod-shaped cells. That's why we can make out shapes and detail in the dark but our vision is almost completely black and white.

There are a handful of sensible precautions to take before venturing out on a night walk in the country: get to know the route in daylight first; make a note of features and landmarks to help you navigate in the dark; pick a mild, rain-free night; and take a back-pack with some warm clothes, a snack, a flask of hot tea and a mobile phone. It's not a bad idea to ask a walking buddy to join you, either. A bit of preparation will reap rewards as a new, nocturnal world opens up. When our normal daytime vision is reduced, the other senses are heightened and even a slight breeze on your face will feel different.

Some of the best locations for a winter night walk also happen to be officially recognised as Dark Sky Parks or Reserves. Snowdonia, the Brecon Beacons, the Yorkshire Dales, the North York Moors, Cranborne Chase, Exmoor, the South Downs and Northumberland National Park are among the places given special status by the International Dark-Sky Association as some of the finest places in the world to see the night sky, free of light pollution. In fact, Northumberland proudly boasts that it has the most pristine dark skies in England and on a really clear cloudless night in the National Park it's possible to see the Andromeda galaxy, two and a half million light years away, with the naked eye.

While you're outside winter stargazing, the darkness provides an ideal opportunity to stop looking for a moment and start listening. My dad taught me and my sisters to identify animal noises when we were young and I still love to stop and listen out for the sounds of wildlife. An owl hooting in the darkness is an obvious one, and I'm sure I hear them far more frequently than I did in the 1980s and '90s. The classic *tu-whit tu-whoo* is the tawny owl, the sound that Shakespeare's 'staring owl which nightly sings' makes in *Love's Labour's Lost*, and for us one of the star voices in the nocturnal choir. Shakespeare was a little mistaken on this though because no owl actually calls *tu-whit tu-whoo*. What the great man heard was, in fact, two tawny owls, the male calling *hoo-hoo* and the female replying *ke-wick*. Shakespeare didn't just get it wrong, he got it back-to-front! I rarely see a tawny but I hear them all the time when they're perching up in the trees. That's their favourite hunting perch, looking down at whatever tasty meal might be scurrying or hopping about around below – a mouse or possibly a frog – before pouncing from on high.

Unlike the tawny, barn owls hunt on the wing, patrolling up and down grassy rides looking for shrews and short-tailed voles. The barn owl is the original screech owl with a hoarse, wheezy wail which sounds more like a pained mammal than a beautiful bird. And they *are* beautiful, with their heart-shaped faces and soft white feathers. Growing up on a farm in a stunning location meant that we were very popular when our relatives from London wanted somewhere to stay. But after dark, my cousins from the capital really didn't enjoy our little corner of the countryside at all. They were used to street lights so didn't like the dark, and when they heard the screeching of barn owls and the distant barking of foxes on the prowl, they virtually refused to leave the house. I was a bit bemused by it all, but I'm sure they're over it now! I hope so, because these days there's a big drive to encourage farmers to put up barn owl nesting boxes in their outdoor buildings, and hundreds have done just that. The reason is that barn owls are an indicator species; their presence indicates great biodiversity and a healthy food chain in the surrounding fields. It means there's rough, grassy habitat with shoots and hedge fruit, which supports small mammals like voles and shrews which, in turn, are food for the owls.

Winter is also a good time to enjoy the silence of the night, as so many of the insects and amphibians which usually create a nocturnal chorus have died away or are hibernating, and there's no better time to lean into that feeling of stillness and quiet than after a fall of snow. Did you know that the magic stillness snow seemingly creates has its roots in science? A blanket of thick snow absorbs sound because snow-flakes are porous – they have open spaces within their crystals – which means they soak up soundwaves. Although no amount of snow can silence the sound of our tractors as we try to carve a way through it to get to the livestock in the fields!

Identify footprints in the snow

When it snows on the top of the Cotswolds, it falls hard and it stays around for weeks and sometimes even months. Nothing moves, cars are abandoned or left in garages, and there's no way a country bus or a home delivery van is going to make it through the drifts. That's when the Hensons play nature detective by looking for animal footprints in the snow. I was taught how to identify wild creatures from their prints by my dad and I did exactly the same with my kids, Ella and Alfie. They're grown up now, but I hope that when the time comes, they'll pass the knowledge on to their children.

The best time of day to look for prints is early in the morning or late in the afternoon when shadows make the impressions easier to see. A keen eye and a bit of luck should reveal the roaming secrets of Britain's favourite mammals:

Picture	Description
fox	A fox print will be roughly diamond-shaped and made up of four toes – two at the front and one each side – with an oval pad at the rear, and their marks will be in a straight line across the snow.
badger	A badger leaves five toe prints with clearly visible claw marks and a broad rear pad.
rabbit	Rabbits leave two sets of prints – long, thin marks from their hind feet and much shorter ones from their forefeet – with four pads on each.

All the deer species in the UK leave similar tracks, so look for two long imprints like an elongated pear with a gap between them.

deer

The snow doesn't just reveal where animals have trekked but also their behaviour. Ella and Alfie were always left open-mouthed when we spotted the fan-shaped dents in the snow caused by the wings of a barn owl, and nearby the tiny footprints of a scurrying mouse which would come to a sudden stop; good news for a hungry owl, bad news for a tasty rodent and a real-life lesson in natural science and survival of the fittest for two inquisitive kids.

11

Walking in Winter: Trees

I don't know if there's a British Tree Appreciation Society, but if there isn't there really should be, because we can all too easily take trees for granted. They're incredibly inspiring things; great for the environment, good for the soul, beautiful to look at, providers of food for wildlife and sanctuaries for nature. I've been planting new trees at Bemborough since the 1990s and across the country hundreds of thousands of saplings go in the ground every year, as we wake up to their importance to life on earth. Planting campaigns have been led by the royal family, in the shape of the Prince of Wales, and broadcasting royalty thanks to the efforts of Sir David Attenborough. Not forgetting the phenomenal response we saw from *Countryfile* viewers when we launched our Plant Britain initiative in 2020 with the hope of achieving 750,000 new tree plantings (one for every child who started primary school that year). We sailed past the target in no time. There's even a new

Countryfile Wood in Cheshire which, in time, will grow into a classic English lowland broadleaf canopy of oak, birch, hornbeam and sweet chestnut.

Although as the saying goes, 'The best time to plant a tree is twenty years ago', better now than never, I guess! That's certainly the spirit behind an innovative trial I visited in the deep, rich soil of Devon where saplings are being planted in fields and meadows where livestock graze. The idea is that when they mature, the trees will improve the environment by capturing carbon, releasing oxygen and boosting biodiversity through the interdependent species they'll attract such as birds, insects and small mammals. At the same time the branches, leaves, fruit and nuts will benefit the sheep and cattle by providing a new food source, natural shelter and somewhere to scratch and rub which does wonders for their skin and general health. It's called silvopasture and there's definitely more scientific research behind this long-term trial than the centuries-old agricultural system of wood pasture where cattle and ponies were released into existing woodland to graze (Epping Forest in Essex is a good example of ancient English wood pasture). Sure enough, the experts in Devon tell me they should know if their silvopasture project has been successful in about twenty years from now.

We appreciate trees most in summer when they're in full leaf, and in autumn when they burst into colour, but there's a heck of a lot to see in winter because the bare branches give us the best opportunity to witness what's going on underneath. That's why I've devoted this last walking section to trees and what to look for in winter.

The first challenge is whether you can work out what sort of tree you're looking at when there are no leaves to help identify it. Looking at the bark on the trunk is often your only clue and once you start, it becomes obvious just how much variety exists from species to species.

The bark protects a tree like a skin, shielding it from the cold, rain, wildlife, pests and disease. It also regulates moisture, keeping the inner sapwood and heartwood dry in wet weather and hydrated when conditions are hot and dry.

Trees expand and grow as they get older; how bark reacts to the aging process differs and depends on what's most important to the particular tree variety. For example, trees with cracked bark like oak tend to be able to grow – and repair wounds – quickly. But the crevices allow insects to enter and the oak has to exert energy in making its bark unpalatable to the intruders to prevent it being attacked. Trees with smooth bark aren't at risk of invading insects in the same way, but keeping the surface flat and level takes up more energy which means the tree usually grows more slowly.

Here are a few types of trees to identify in winter from their bark alone:

Type of tree	Description
wild cherry tree	To be found all over Britain, though less frequently in Northern Ireland, the wild cherry's bark has lovely 'tiger stripes' on it – short straight scars on its surface that are actually lenticels. Lenticels are pores that allow gases from the air to get through to the internal tissues of the tree. Apart from this, the wild cherry's bark is smooth with a reddish-brown colour reminiscent of its fruit.
London plane	Although most commonly found in the south-east of England, the London plane grows all over and its bark has a unique appearance: it looks a little like camouflage because the greyish-green outer layer peels away in sections to reveal paler colours underneath. This shedding is to protect itself from air pollutants, soot, fungi, parasites, mosses and lichen.
silver birch	One of the easiest trees to identify from its bark, because, like the tree's name, it's silver in colour. It's not smooth, however; you'll see black fissures along its surface and the more of these you can see, the older the tree is likely to be.

Towards the end of winter, you can start trying to identify trees from their buds. Some of the easiest to spot are oak, ash and sycamore. Oak trees have orange-brown buds, a similar colour to their acorns, with blunt or rounded ends which sit in clusters on the ends of the twigs. If the leaf buds are black and feel like velvet on the end of grey twigs, it'll be an ash tree. Buds that are lime green, exactly the same colour as the boiled lime sweets we had as kids, arranged in opposite pairs with a slightly larger bud at the end, belong to the sycamore.

A couple more for luck. If you have a trusty horse chestnut which dropped its crop of conkers a few months ago, check out its buds in winter. These are a glossy, sticky brown which show green growth just before the first leaves appear. Finally, the magnificent magnolia makes it easy for the amateur tree-spotter – in the last half of winter many varieties have big, plump flower buds covered in little soft white or grey hairs.

Looking at bark and buds aren't the only ways to identify trees in winter, though. So long as you're not harming the tree – don't go upsetting any new growth – interacting with trees can help. The crack willow, which can be found all over the UK, has brittle twigs that make a noticeable 'crack' sound if you break them. It's most often alongside rivers or lakes and has a very craggy trunk, so if you spot one that fits the bill, why not give a twig a snap?

Apart from things on the tree, there are several things that appear *in* trees in winter that are worth spotting. You might spy an untidy mass of old leaves and twigs mixed with moss, grass and even a feather or two – like a large, badly made bird's nest. A nest is exactly what it is, but it belongs to a squirrel, not a bird. Squirrel nests, or dreys, are normally seen in the forks of branches or in a hole within the trunk, built from whatever they can gather to keep them warm, dry and safe. This winter home might be an adapted summer drey – which is flatter and lighter because it needs less protection from the elements – or it might be a new nest they've built for themselves in preparation for the arrival of a litter of young (called kits or kittens), which are often born towards the end of winter, in February. If you're still unsure, look for scratch marks on the bark or chewed pine cones littered about under the tree; that'll be the squirrel's work. There are two types of squirrel in the UK – the native red and the grey which was introduced from North America in the 1800s – but they both make the same type of nest.

Another nest-like structure that can be found in trees all year round, but only becomes visible in winter when the leaves have dropped, is an unusual and pretty unmistakable thing called 'witches' broom': the perfect description of the tangled woody shoots, stems and roots which grow untidily from a single point, just as if a flying witch has crash-landed in the middle of the trunk. In fact, it's a deformity which can happen anywhere in trees, caused by tiny fungal growths or by viral, bacterial or insect activity, which make the buds produce uncontrolled stems. It sounds nasty, but it doesn't stop the tree growing and if it takes hold in an orchard, the fruit won't be affected.

If you spot witches' broom in winter, it's worth going back in spring and summer to see how much of it you can see when the leaves and blossom are out.

Something else that's caused by viral or fungal infection are burrs – that's the name for the large knobbly lumps that grow on the side of trees. They can also grow underground, at the base of the trunk and on the branches. Burrs are rather clever: they're made up of bud and shoot tissue which responds under stress to protect the tree from further damage and, despite looking a bit warty, they don't cause any harm in themselves. In fact, there are lots of carpenters and craftsmen who go out of their way to find wood with unusual grain patterns caused by burrs and customers seem to like it too. There's a living to be had from using burr-damaged wood to make furniture, knife handles and even the polished wooden dashboards of expensive sports cars.

Identifying tree species, and noting the tell-tale signs of life in the bark and the branches, is almost a hobby in its own right. But the next level of tree appreciation is all about speculation: do you know enough about botany to age a tree?

There are some unbelievably old trees in every county of the kingdom, including one I drive past every time I travel to the *Countryfile* office at BBC Bristol. The Tortworth Chestnut, not far from the M5 in Gloucestershire, is tucked away in the corner of a field just a short walk from the door of the local parish church. How old is it? Well, an old plaque dated 1 January 1800 states that the tree was six hundred years old then, but some records claim it grew from a nut planted in the days of King Egbert in the year 800. That would make it more than 1,200 years old. Unfortunately, it's impossible to get an accurate idea of its age; the huge trunk is too gnarly and old branches have rooted and regrown in their own right. But I don't need to know; I like the mystery and wonder surrounding this monumental living landmark.

The best way to age a tree is the tried and tested method we all learnt about at school: count the rings. Trees put on a layer of growth every year so the trunk of a felled tree will have a series of dark rings through it. Starting nearest the pith at the centre and working out to the bark, the number of these rings you count will equal the age of the tree in years. Experts can also work out the climate at certain points in history because the thicker the rings, the better the growing conditions were that year. Of course, no tree surgeon wants to chop down a healthy specimen just to work out how old it is, which is where boring bars come in. They work just like cheese irons, to take a plug of wood from the main trunk for analysis.

Seeing that you're not going to chop down a tree or use a boring bar in the middle of a winter walk (let's leave that to the experts), the cheat's way of working out the age of a standing tree is to look at how wide it is. If it's very wide – or if the main trunk seems to have split into two trunks at the bottom – then there's a good chance it's very aged or even ancient.

What you'll hopefully find if you do get out and age a tree is that our countryside is full of specimens that have been growing for many decades and, in some cases, centuries. Trees connect us with people from the past – a Celt from 1,000 BC might not recognise much about our modern lifestyle, but they would be at home among the aspen, oak and alder trees that have grown in Britain and Ireland for thousands of years. It's comforting to think that the outline of familiar trees on the horizon has been largely unchanged down the ages. The reason there are so few ancient examples like the Tortworth Chestnut is because, like humans, trees age and die – and of course since the Middle Ages we've cleared huge areas of forest and woodland to make space for agriculture and the growth of industrial towns and cities. We've also cut down trees because we've found many uses for different types of wood over the years. Hornbeam is a good tree for wildlife in winter because, while its leaves turn brown, they don't drop (this is known as marcescence, which means 'to fade' in Latin, referring to the colour of the leaves). The name hornbeam comes from 'beam', the Old English word for 'tree', with 'horn' referring to the toughness of the wood, which is so hardy it was considered closer to the horn of an animal. It's why hornbeam was used to make ox yokes; where other wood might break under the pressure of the oxen pulling the plough, hornbeam was tough and sturdy.

I have a special fondness for beech trees because so many of them grow on the farm and across the Cotswolds. They're local landmarks in this open, rural landscape and at the top of the paddock, not far from my house, there's one particular group of beech trees called Buttington Clump. It's visible for miles around and ever since my sisters and I were little, it's been a welcome sign that we're nearly home. Even now, when I'm driving back after a long day's work or a filming assignment for *Countryfile*, I'm always happy when Buttington Clump comes into view and I know I'm almost at journey's end.

The Romans rated beech as firewood so highly they burned it to smelt iron, and in the seventeenth century its leaves were used to create poultices and its tar to make an antiseptic. Meanwhile sycamore is still used to fashion Welsh love spoons (those decoratively carved romantic gifts), and the sap was used to make ale in days gone by.

Other tree traditions have withstood the test of time. If there's a cider apple orchard near you, there's a good chance that at some point a wassail has taken place there, especially if you're in the Midlands or the south and west of England, and this annual celebration is making a comeback. Like so many calendar events in this country, its roots are way back in pre-Christian times, and the word itself is Old English. *Waes Haell* meant 'be healthy' and survives today when drinkers wish each other 'good health'. Wassailing the apple trees is all about warding off evil spirits and encouraging the trees to produce a healthy crop in the coming year. One evening after dark, early in the New Year, bonfires are lit in a circle, toast is lodged in the branches as an offering to the spirits and the last of the previous year's cider is poured round the base of a tree. There's a lot of singing, banging of drums, clattering of saucepans and drinking (of course)! Sometimes a shotgun is fired through the branches of the trees to send the devil on his way. It sounds slightly mad, but it's all done very knowingly and with more and more wassails taking place every year, it's becoming a very sociable way of brightening up the dark days of January. Keep an eye on the local press or look for posters in garden centres and farm shops for details of your nearest wassail. It's a great excuse to get close to trees, discover more about their importance to local life and taste the fruit at its heady, golden, lip-smacking best.

The Christmas robin

The symbol of winter is *Erithacus rubecula,* known to everyone as the robin; the star of a million Christmas cards, calendars and tea-towels. It's odd that the robin has become associated with the festive season because they're resident in the UK all year round and the connection with Christmas only came about by accident. Victorian postmen wore red uniforms which earned them the nickname Red Breasts, so it wasn't much of a leap when stationers began printing pictures of robins on the Christmas cards that were delivered to homes in their millions every December.

I love to see robins sitting on the wall behind our house and if I'm taking a break from digging the garden there's a fair chance I'll return to see a brave robin perched on the handle of the fork or even hopping along the ground heading for the back door. They're obviously fearless and always appear friendly, which along with their instantly recognisable bright colouring explains their popularity – they've frequently topped polls for the nation's favourite bird. The truth is that the robin is actually a bit of a brute! A pair of male robins will fight to the death in the battle over territory and that's why it sings all year round – to tell other birds to back off!

I know a few people who think of lost family members when they see a robin and although I'm not sure

I believe in reincarnation, I do the same and always think about my dad. If I'm out working on the farm and I notice a nearby robin looking on, I'll always give it a smile and a nod. There may be nothing in it, but it gives me comfort and reminds me of all the things Dad taught me about the joys of the natural world. We haven't always called the robin by its familiar name. Originally it was called 'rudduc' from the Anglo-Saxon for 'little red one', then in the Middle Ages when common creatures were given human nicknames it became 'Robert' Ruddock. Robert was eventually shortened to Robin, although until the early twentieth century most people just called it a red-breast.

12

The Winter Solstice

Want to observe the oldest winter celebration in the world? That'll be the winter solstice, which usually occurs on 21 December (in the northern hemisphere), the shortest day of the year, which is also known as Yule. It probably goes back to the earliest ancient people who hunted and spent most of the year outside, so the seasons played a huge part in their lives. The early solstice celebrations involved worshipping the sun and willing it to return. Celts, Romans and Vikings added layers of custom to the ritual such as processions, lighting candles and exchanging presents. Many of those elements were adapted or incorporated wholesale into early Christmas celebrations.

A popular way to celebrate the solstice is to bring greenery indoors by decorating your house with sprigs of holly and bunches of mistletoe. This is a tradition at this time of year which goes back to the Druids and the Celts – a pagan ritual associated with evergreens being sacred and linked to everlasting life. Traditionally people connected holly with weather: if the tree bears a plentiful supply of berries then we're in for a hard winter and if you grow holly beside your house it was thought to protect against thunder and lightning. As for gathering mistletoe, that began with the Romans who thought it represented peace, love and understanding, so they started hanging it over doorways to protect the home and everyone inside it. Things got spicier with the Celts and druids who saw it as a fertility symbol, believing that the white berries contained the spirit of the tree. So we have them to thank for the tradition of kissing loved ones – and strangers – underneath the mistletoe.

Today the best place to buy mistletoe is the annual Tenbury Wells auction in Worcestershire, which proudly declares itself 'The Mistletoe Capital of England'. And well it might because not only is this riverside town in the heart of the mistletoe-growing region, its Christmas market dates back more than 160 years and there's a very festive, carnival feel when the crowds gather for the bidding.

If you prefer to harvest your own mistletoe, it's relatively easy to do if you're comfortable using a ladder or telescopic shears and you've got the permission of the landowner. Mistletoe is a parasitic plant (once described by *National Geographic* magazine as 'everyone's favourite parasite'). It doesn't kill the tree it lives on but survives by absorbing the nutrients and water of the host. It's particularly fond of apple trees, poplars, willow, birch, hazel, lime and maple where it grows in large green orbs which hang on the bare branches. Mistletoe is protected under the same law that governs all wild plants in the UK, which means you can pick it but removing the entire plant is an offence.

As well as bringing nature indoors, why not put a Yule log on your shopping list – not a chocolate Swiss roll, but a log for burning. Yule is a Viking word connected to the solstice; the Vikings thought that the sun stopped moving in the sky, believing that the flaming star in the heavens rested, so to combat their fear of eternal winter they lit fires to encourage the sun to come back to life. The fires were kept burning until they noticed the days beginning to lengthen again, about twelve days later; which fits very neatly into our own twelve days of Christmas and the tradition of keeping a Yule log alight the entire time. Across Northern Europe and Scandinavia softwood conifers were used, but here harder, more substantial ash or oak logs were lit and when we revived the Yule log custom in the 1600s, there are stories of trees so big that teams of horses were needed to pull the timber from the forests up to the local manor or large farmhouses where gangs of farm labourers would drag it in through the great hall and into the huge open fire where it would blaze away from Christmas Eve until Twelfth Night. The log served another purpose for the superstitious Georgians – they liked to 'burn away' their faults and mistakes of the previous year by writing all their errors down on paper and ceremoniously throwing them into the flames. Give it a try – who knows, it might even work!

For our prehistoric ancestors, the winter solstice would have been accompanied by drinking and feasting. At a time when famine and starvation were common, cattle and pigs were routinely slaughtered to save them having to be fed through the worst of the winter weather. It meant there was a ready supply of fresh meat as well as beer and wine made earlier in the year and fermented in time for the solstice festivities. Today the idea of a communal banquet so close to Christmas Day would be impractical – although the butcher and the wine merchant I know in Stow-on-the-Wold would love it.

If you fancy marking the winter solstice in style, you could do a lot worse than joining the festivities at Stonehenge. The Neolithic landmark in Wiltshire is well known for the celebrations at sunrise on the summer solstice in June, but the ancient sarsen stones are also aligned with sunset on the winter solstice. The ancients who built the henge knew that the turning point of the sun's passage in the heavens in winter was just as important as the one in midsummer. So do many modern-day pilgrims, pagans and druids who regard the site as sacred and gather there every year for the first sunrise after the longest night (albeit in smaller numbers than the six thousand or more who crowd around the stones in summer). In recent years old beliefs and new technology have merged with the event streamed live on the internet.

There are dozens of songs and poems which tell a story of long, drawn-out winter months, but I always think the season flies by. There must be other farmers who feel exactly the same. The run-up to Christmas is always frenetic with family plans for the holiday, a big influx of visitors to the Farm Park keen to meet Santa and his elves, and filming the all-important *Countryfile* festive special as well as getting several editions of the programme 'in the can' for the New Year.

When January arrives there are just six weeks before we open the gates to the public again for the new season, and with hundreds of pregnant ewes to care for along with the numerous rare breed sheep, cattle, pigs and horses to look after, there's no time for slacking. Here and on farms all over the country, January and February are when essential repairs and renovations take place. Now, that might be something as simple as mending a broken fence, but it could easily mean re-roofing barns, replacing underground pipes or constructing entirely new outbuildings.

Winter might be the quietest time of year for nature and wildlife, but for me those months are a blur. Soon I start to notice the sun shining a little stronger, the daylight lasting a little longer and the birdsong sounding a little louder. Even when there are still pockets of hard, frozen snow defiantly refusing to thaw in ditches and tyre tracks on the farm, the signs are all pointing to the imminent arrival of spring.

The Farmer's Diary

Here's what you can expect to see from farmers during winter:

	Arable farming	Livestock farming
December	Arable crops lay dormant for the winter. Recently harvested winter vegetables are in season – parsnips, swede, cauliflowers, leeks and beetroot. In field boundaries, coppicing and hedgelaying are underway.	As temperatures drop, livestock feed rations are adjusted to give them the right balance of protein, vitamins and minerals for winter. Cattle markets everywhere stage their annual Fatstock Sales. Turkeys and geese are plucked and prepared for Christmas.
January	Traditionally the quietest time of the year so an opportunity to repair and replace gates, fences and farm buildings. Farm machinery is serviced. In commercial orchards, tree pruning begins.	Especially on northern farms, fodder root crops are fed to sheep. In the south the first ewes give birth to produce early lamb in time for Easter.
February	The first crops of the new year are drilled (planted) – spring wheat, barley and oats.	The Farm Park reopens with live lambing and kidding demonstrations in the Animal Barn.

Five other things
to see or do in winter

1. Help animals in need

I remember one particularly bad winter in the 1970s
when the white-out meant none of the stockmen
could get to the farm, so feeding the livestock became
a family affair with me and my sisters helping Dad.
This was long before the advent of four-wheel drive
all-terrain vehicles, and even if they had existed the
snow was so deep, I think they would have struggled.
Luckily we had a strong and sturdy Shire horse called
Kitty and with an up-turned Morris Minor chassis
from the scrapheap attached to her harness, we had a
brilliant improvised horse-drawn sledge. We loaded
it with hay and Kitty took us down the frozen farm
tracks and across the snowbound fields to get to all
the animals stranded in the drifts. At one point the

snow was so deep that Kitty was able to scramble over a wall, dragging us behind her, and I can remember lots of laughing as we fell off the makeshift sledge. No risk assessments or health and safety inspections in those days!

But there was a serious side to our adventure. A well-tended farm or an isolated hamlet of cottages looks picturesque in the heady days of spring and summer, but the hardship of winter is not to be underestimated. Frozen pipes and water troughs can take hours to thaw out, taking up precious time when livestock need more attention than usual. Food, water and shelter are the basics of animal husbandry, with a secure enclosure to guarantee protection, but all those things are compromised by freezing temperatures and heavy snow.

Sheep can stay hydrated by eating snow, although cattle are less keen and keeping water supplied to pigs reared outdoors is a major headache to pork farmers. The only way to keep them all watered and the field pipes flowing is to use a blow-torch, digging down in to the ground below the frost line and making sure to avoid melting any plastic fittings. It can seem like an endless, thankless job and in the very worst weather the water can freeze again within half an hour and it's back to square one. It must be done though.

It's not only farm animals which need help; wild mammals are hit just as hard by bad weather. I leave upturned bin lids filled with water next to the troughs and along some of the farm tracks. Squirrels will still venture into gardens at this time of year, especially if you have peanuts and scraps scattered around a bird table, and if you notice that snow, soil or leaf litter has been disturbed in the night then you'll have had a visit from a badger, in search of a meal. The same is true of foxes, looking for food, although they'll be much lighter on their feet. We think of our own individual gardens as places for wildlife, but birds don't see a single outdoor space in isolation, they visit a collection of gardens and treat it as one large habitat. At this time of year flocks of great, blue and long-tailed tits, tree creepers and an occasional nuthatch will work their way through a row of adjoining gardens, looking for food in bushes and trees or dipping a beak into the birdbath, before fluttering up and over the fence on their whistle-stop tour of the neighbourhood. Give them a helping hand with a well-stocked bird feeder in your yard or garden, some fat-balls hanging from the bird table and a couple of places where there's clean, fresh water.

2. Track otter droppings

Anything to do with snow will keep a child occupied, but as every parent knows, little ones are even more fascinated by poo. And when the snows have melted, exposing the bare ground again, animal droppings are a thing of wonder. The Cotswold rivers which trickle from the cold hills down to the stripling Thames have wonderful names: the Churn, Coln, Dickler and Evenlode, not forgetting the most famous of all the tributaries, the Windrush. For my money it's got the best, most evocative name of any river in Britain and lucky for me, it flows through our farm. More importantly it is home to one of our loveliest and most elusive mammals, the otter.

People often confuse otters with beavers, probably because they're both water-loving mammals, but that's where the similarity ends. Otters are long, sleek creatures with a powerful pointed tail, grey-brown fur, a pale chest and a broad snout. Beavers are much bulkier and are Britain's biggest rodent, so imagine a large mouse or rat, about the size of a small dog, and you won't be far off. Their densely packed fur is brown or black and the distinctive feature is their tail – it's broad and flat like a paddle. Their diet couldn't be more unlike an otter's; they're herbivores so you'll never find them eating fish.

I would love to see an otter in the wild and every time I'm near the Windrush I hold my breath in hope, but so far the nearest I've come is discovering otter spraints (the polite way of saying otter poo). Wintertime, when the riverbank vegetation is low, is the ideal time to look for evidence of them. They're black, slimy and absolutely stink of fish. If you want to get your hands dirty and examine one further, you'll find scales, bones, bits of shell and insects in an undigested tarry mess. You might be put off by the sight and smell, but don't underestimate the importance of otter spraint to wildlife conservation. They are remarkably shy creatures and trying to establish population numbers from sightings and head counts is impossible – so detailed recordings of their droppings are crucial to mapping the otter across the country. It helps that they don't hibernate or have a specific breeding season and they return to the same places to mark their territory. Wooden logs, old stones and under bridges are favourite spots to find a half-digested fishy deposit.

3. Take part in the Big Garden Birdwatch

If you're anything like me you'll love seeing the birds flit and flutter about in the garden, pulling worms from the ground or taking a dust bath (which is vital to stop a bird's feathers from becoming too oily and matted). We've come to rely on scientists and experts to tell us how our wildlife is coping, the latest population figures and what species are under threat. But when it comes to birds, gathering the raw data is in our hands. The RSPB can't send an officer out with a clipboard to do a survey of the birdlife in every street in the country, so instead it runs the Big Garden Birdwatch every January. Anyone who loves nature is asked to spend an hour noting down which birds visit their garden and sending the results in. It's what they call citizen science and with about a million people taking part every year, it's the largest wildlife study in the world.

For such a big event, it had modest beginnings. The first Birdwatch took place in 1979 as a project for children and launched on the BBC programme *Blue Peter*. Of course, in those days the kids had to post their results to Television Centre – the internet was the stuff of science fiction. We always take part at home and if you like the idea too, you can find out more online at rspb.org.uk or look for the guides and bird ID charts in newspapers and magazines in the New Year.

4. Spot the signs of love

People have been falling in love for as long as there have been people! So naturally there are endless superstitions, predictions and omens about finding (and losing) your sweetheart, and more of these beliefs in country districts than anywhere else. Some are firmly consigned to the past, but one or two others are just waiting for a romantic revival. For instance, the first recipe for single women wanting to know the identity of their future husband was published in the 1600s. And it was literally a recipe. The unmarried maiden was told to bake a 'dumb cake' on Christmas Eve (and other red letter days through the year such as New Year's Eve, Midsummer and Hallowe'en). It was made by mixing together an eggshell of salt, one of malt and one of barley meal (sounds delicious!) but the magical ingredient was total silence. Without saying a word she would put the mixture in a pan over the fire, turning it as it cooked. That's when a vision of the man she would marry would mysteriously appear.

In the north of England there was also a rhyme which had to be recited:

O good St Faith, be kind to-night
And bring to me my heart's delight;
Let me my future husband view,
And be my visions chaste and true.

If you're unlucky in love, it might be worth giving it a try. If that doesn't work, wait for the first new moon of the New Year. The next night, as the moon appears, look at it through a silk handkerchief. The number of moons you see through the fabric is said to predict the number of months (or new moons) that will pass before you meet your true love.

A special occasion which always gives a bit of a boost in winter is St Valentine's Day. In folklore it's thought that birds begin to pair on 14 February and women are advised to take special note of the first bird which flies overhead that morning. If it's a robin, the tradition states she'll marry a sailor, if it's a goldfinch her husband will be a rich man and a sparrow means he'll be a poor man but one who makes her happy.

Once you've found that true love, you need to pick up a swan feather. As mute swans mate for life, it's believed that sewing one of their feathers on the inside of your sweetheart's pillowcase will ensure they remain faithful to you.

5. Seek out snowdrops

The closing weeks of winter bring hopes of warmer, brighter times ahead with the arrival of snowdrops. Once Christmas has come and gone, I patiently wait for the show of snowdrops to appear beneath the beech trees in our garden. They always remind me of my mum, who moved into the farmhouse with Dad in 1962, and loved these very plants with their tiny cheerful flowers. It was something about the bright white petals emerging at the darkest, greyest time of the year that appealed to her, I think. When you live on an escarpment eight hundred feet above sea level, it's not unusual for the snowdrops to push through a frozen covering of snow before they show themselves, and Mum must have seen that promising display of white-on-white dozens of times over the decades.

So you can imagine how thrilled I was when *Countryfile* sent me on a filming assignment to the two finest snowdrop collections in the land. The pretty village of Painswick is known as 'The Queen of the Cotswolds' with its attractive narrow streets, a stunning fourteenth-century church and a famous collection of ninety-nine yew trees in the churchyard – legend has it that all attempts to grow a hundredth tree end in failure and the extra yew always dies. No such mysterious goings-on nearby at the Rococo Gardens though, where I was greeted by a carpet of majestic snowdrops. The wooded glades and steep banks are in the grounds of stately Painswick House which were laid out in the 1700s as a pleasure garden for the well-to-do. Today they are home to five million snowdrops which are so densely packed that they look, from a distance, like a spotless covering of virgin snow.

If that wasn't breath-taking enough, my next stop was Colesbourne Park in the beautiful Churn valley midway between Cheltenham and Cirencester. The whole estate is 2,500 acres with two farms, nine hundred acres of forestry, an arboretum, a lake and various buildings in the village. But every year

Colesbourne is transformed into a botanical 'must-see'. It's here that Sir Henry Elwes and his wife, Lady Carolyn, play host to thousands of visitors every January and February when, for a brief few weeks, ten acres of private grounds and woodland walks are completely taken over by the delicate white flowers. There are about 350 varieties including many which are derived from originals planted by Sir Henry's great-grandfather, the famed Victorian traveller and plantsman H. J. Elwes. Enthusiastic snowdrop collectors are officially known as galanthophiles – a word that came in very useful recently when I spent a day hiking in the Brecon Beacons to celebrate a friend's fiftieth birthday. Among the group was a keen snowdrop fan and when I mentioned that I liked them too, he insisted that we walk together for the rest of the day: 'We galanthophiles must stick together!'

Painswick Rococo Gardens opens daily when the first snowdrops come into flower (usually late January) while Colesbourne Park usually welcomes visitors for five consecutive weekends between January and the end of February. Plan a visit – you won't be disappointed.

Farewell

The blizzard of sweetly scented snowdrops is over quickly, but they'll soon be replaced by crocuses, then the welcome sight of the yellow-trumpeted daffodils ... and so the passage of the seasons comes full circle. The sunshine follows the thaw, buds appear on the bare branches, the dark hour before dawn lifts with the first songbirds again. If there's one thing we can rely on, it's that summer will always follow spring and after every autumn mist comes a winter chill, with new discoveries and a sense of wonder at every turn.

Recently I read a very interesting article by disability ambassador Tom Jamison about the UK's most sensational outdoor experiences, which highlighted the ways in which the natural world can be enjoyed by people with sight, smell or hearing loss and other sensory impairments. It included the textures of lichen, ferns and tree bark on a woodland stroll, the invigorating rush of cold water when wild swimming and the closeness of nature on a river fishing trip, as well as the daily phenomena of sunrise and sunset. It's something I've thought a lot about at the Farm Park over the years. For decades we've welcomed visitors who have health conditions, impairments and disabilities of many kinds and it's a privilege to wait and watch as they interact with our animals; hand feeding our greedy goats, holding a fluffy chick for the first time or helping to bottle-feed a newborn lamb in the discovery barn. But Tom made me think deeper about other, less obvious, experiences which take place on the farm every day. The tingle of the breeze against the face on a stroll up the gentle incline to the top of the animal paddocks, the scents drifting across the pathways through the flower field when it's full of wild blooms and the calming effect of watching bees at work producing honey in the specially built glass-fronted observation hive. Proof, if it were needed, that the great outdoors is a full-on sensory experience.

We can't deny that climate change is having an impact on our seasons and that we need to work quickly if we're going to halt its effects – but among the warning signs there's good news which shows that, with a little help, nature can fight back. For instance, some of our favourite birds are on the up, with jays and greenfinches flocking back to our gardens in numbers not seen in decades. The results of the Big Garden Birdwatch in 2022 saw a 73 per cent year-on-year increase in jay sightings and an 8 per cent rise in greenfinch numbers. The long-term trends for other birds are encouraging too; blue tit, great tit and goldfinch populations are up over the last forty years or so. Even species on the very brink of extinction are getting a helping hand. Black-tailed godwits are long-legged, beaky wading birds and in 2017 there were fewer than fifty breeding pairs in the entire UK, on just two sites in East Anglia. But after a hand-rearing programme called 'Project Godwit' was launched by conservation charities, more than two hundred birds were released in Cambridgeshire and Norfolk.

There are reasons to feel optimistic about other creatures, even pollinators whose decline has caused so much concern recently. In 2022 the ruderal bumblebee, a species which was thought to be extinct in Wales, was spotted in Carmarthenshire for the first time since 1973. Families of beavers have returned to the River Otter in Devon and to Cropton Forest in North Yorkshire after successful reintroductions, while in Scotland the beaver population has doubled in recent years. The distinctive long-legged, big-beaked great crane is back from extinction in Britain and its trumpeting call can be heard again on the Somerset levels and moors after a six-year programme of hatching and rearing in south-west England.

I'm also heartened by the interest children have in food, farming and the countryside in general. It's marvellous to see. Every day I meet kids, sometimes only just old enough to be at school, who are entirely engaged with rare breeds. They'll recite back to me facts about Berkshire pigs or Dexter cattle, and ask me genuinely informed questions about their favourite animals at the Farm Park; Lexy the Suffolk Punch horse or the offspring of our Highland bull, Black Prince. Meanwhile for young people in their teens and twenties, rural studies have never been more popular and every year the agricultural colleges are over-subscribed. In the early 1950s, my dad studied for his farming diploma at the Royal Agricultural College in Cirencester, at a time when similar institutions were packed with the sons of high-ranking army officers, top civil servants and the landed gentry. Today the college is a world-renowned university, attracting budding entrepreneurs from all walks of life and from every corner of the globe. It's also a place that debunks the idea that agriculture and land management are careers for men. The latest figures show that Cirencester's students are 52 per cent female. When they graduate they'll join the ranks of farm managers, agri-business people, wildlife conservationists, animal scientists and vets whose expertise is making a difference on a daily basis.

Then there are the fortunes of our native farm livestock. If you'd have asked me a few years ago about Albion cattle, the old county breed of Derbyshire, I'd have said it died out in the 1960s when the last dwindling herd or two disappeared. Everyone thought the same. They used to be known as Blue Albions, or Bakewell Blues after the spa town where they were popular, and a century ago there were hopes that the breed would be the future of dairying in England. But instead, extinction loomed. Now, thanks to advances in genetic testing, and a little group of isolated cattle breeders whose livestock had been forgotten and unrecorded, we know that this docile beef and dairy breed survived all along, albeit in tiny numbers. I'm very proud to have set up a breeding herd and played a role in putting the pride of Derbyshire back on the map.

And everywhere increasing numbers of farmers are doing more for nature than ever before. Agriculture is changing and the way farming is funded is changing too, with the biggest rewards out in the fields and meadows: birds, bees, bugs and butterflies. British farming has a progressively positive story to tell about high standards, excellent welfare, sustainability and a renewed push for better biodiversity and conservation. I'm very proud to say that farmers are the people responsible for ten thousand football pitches' worth of wildflowers, 255,384 miles of hedgerows in England and Wales, and four billion visits by the public to farmed land every single year. Numbers that are growing every day. Those farmers deserve our support and fair prices for the products they produce.

It might be my imagination, but I'm sure there are more wild daffodils growing on the roadsides these days, the clusters of forget-me-nots are bigger and bluer, and the gorse almost ablaze with colour like an avenue of gold. And last spring I could swear the cherry, plum and apple blossom was the loveliest I've ever seen. Mother Nature has a habit of making her presence felt, I suppose, when we give ourselves the time to stop and enjoy the world around us.

Extra Resources

Countryside rights of way

On a country ramble or a serious hike in the hills or dales, it's the walker's responsibility to stay safe, keep within the law and avoid trespassing. But can you be certain what's allowed and what's not? Here's a list of the most common signs and what they mean.

- A yellow arrow is a footpath that's been recorded as a right of way for walkers and people who use mobility aids.
- A blue arrow is a bridleway, which allows horse-riders and cyclists as well as walkers and mobility aid users.
- A purple arrow is a restricted byway, so horse-drawn vehicles are also allowed.

- A red arrow is a byway that's open to every-one and, crucially, that includes motor vehicles. Be warned!
- An acorn symbol on signs and wooden posts marks part of a National Trail. They are designed for walkers with horse-riders and cyclists allowed on some routes. The very nature of these trails means that not all of them are suitable for people with limited mobility but all the access information is on the National Trail website www.nationaltrail.co.uk
- A round brown symbol with an image of a hill walker in the centre means open access and you can venture off pathways. Included are areas of mountain, moors, heathland and registered common land.
- A local sign with the words 'Permissive Path' is a route across private land with access provided voluntarily by the landowner. It's not a right of way and details of who can use the path will be posted alongside.

National Parks, AONBs and SSSIs

There are a number of ways that the countryside and our remarkable open spaces are officially protected.

But the three which most people recognise are National Parks, Areas of Outstanding Natural Beauty and Sites of Special Scientific Interest.

National Parks

There are fifteen National Parks in the UK, which were set up in 1949 to conserve and enhance the natural beauty of our very finest countryside as well as providing recreation for a nation that was still enduring food rationing and post-war austerity.

I particularly love ...

- Brecon Beacons – a magnet for Welsh stargazers with its famously dark skies.
- Exmoor – famous for its trees including the tallest in England, a 197ft /60m Douglas fir near Dunster.
- Yorkshire Dales – England's highest unbroken drop waterfall is Hardraw Force in Wensleydale.

Areas of Outstanding Natural Beauty

There are other parts of the country which are also noted for their special character, abundance of wildlife and importance to the nation, called Areas of Outstanding Natural Beauty (AONBs). There are forty-six of them in England, Wales and Northern Ireland and, broadly similar, forty National Scenic Areas (NSAs) in Scotland.

They include ...

- Causeway Coast – named after Antrim's world-renowned rock columns, the Giant's Causeway.
- Dedham Vale – charming Essex/Suffolk border-land which delighted the artist John Constable.
- Gower – a peninsula of woodland, commons, sandstone and salt marsh in West Glamorgan.

Sites of Special Scientific Interest

There is plenty of overlap with a third category of protection, Sites of Special Scientific Interest (SSSI). They can make up part of a National Park, an ANOB or an NSA and are often small, localised patches of the countryside which are significant for certain species of plants, wildlife or for their special terrain.

Among the best are ...

- Aversley Wood – a haven for wildlife in the UK's least wooded county, Huntingdonshire

- Salmondsbury – the richest and largest traditional hay meadows in the Cotswolds
- Ruislip Woods – near my dad's childhood home in Middlesex, a magnet for swans and geese

I know quite a bit about these protected places because our entire farm falls within the Cotswolds AONB and one corner of it, called Barton Bushes, is an SSSI. So like all farmers, we take specialist advice to make sure nothing we do damages the world-famous landscape.

Country calendar

The countryside has always worked to a calendar. Even before the written word, printed books, clocks and computers, our ancestors were keeping track of time and marking the changing tides, the phases of the moon or the rhythm of the seasons. I said earlier that there's even a theory, backed by academics, that Stonehenge is actually an enormous calendar; a primitive way of tracking a solar year with the ancient monument aligned to the summer and winter solstices, and each of the sarsen stones in the circle representing a day within a month.

Until the eighteenth century we had a different calendar to the one we're familiar with, and a system which essentially went back to the days of Julius Caesar and the Romans. The Julian calendar approximately followed the solar year and New Year's Day was on 25 March. But it was realised that an astronomical error made the calendar year too long and over the course of several centuries the dates of the equinoxes were out of kilter. So a new Gregorian calendar, named after Pope Gregory, put that right and, long after the rest of Europe changed over, Great Britain finally adopted it in 1752. But to catch up we had to lose eleven days, so that year 2 September was followed by 14 September. There was outrage. People were worried they'd lose wages, some thought their lives were being shortened by the government and a story grew up that there were street riots with protestors chanting 'Give us our eleven days.' Even into the twentieth century there were diehards in some rural districts who continued to follow the old calendar, celebrating Christmas Day on 6 January and Twelfth Night on the seventeenth!

The feast days of the saints held incredible importance in country areas for a long time, some for their religious significance, a few because of superstition and others because they were the patron saints of places or professions. A few still strike a chord today, such at St Valentine and St Swithin, not to mention the national saints: David, Patrick, George and Andrew. What would the Six Nations rugby or football's Euro qualifiers be without them? St Piran's popularity as the patron saint of Cornwall never wavered and his feast day is marked with huge celebrations from Launceston to Land's End on 5 March. That sense of local allegiance and county pride is taking off elsewhere with more shires adopting their own special day of the year to promote tourism, food, farming, local heritage, their coast or their countryside. Some, like Devon Day and Oxfordshire Day, are traditional celebrations. Others including Suffolk, Norfolk and Lincolnshire are much more recent, with the dates and events decided not by councils or politicians but chosen at the grass roots by local people to honour their centuries-old historic counties.

So here's my countryside calendar. There are a few important awareness days in there, a smattering of well-known customs as well as the annual celebrations and public holidays you would expect to see. It's impossible to include everything and you will almost certainly know a rural tradition, event or ritual that's local to you.

January

First Sunday after 6 January – Plough
Sunday (a church celebration to mark the

agricultural New Year)

First Monday after 6 January – Plough Monday (the day when farm labourers returned to the fields after Christmas)

6 – Old Christmas Day (Julian calendar)

17 – Old Twelfth Night (Julian calendar)

29 – National Potato Day (launched in 1994 to promote the Great British spud)

February

2 – Candlemas (the mid-point of winter marked in church by the blessing of candles)

14 – St Valentine's Day

29 – Leap Year Day (every fourth year)

March

First Sunday after the first full moon following the spring equinox – Easter

Forty-six days before Easter – Lent begins

Third Thursday in March – Kiplingcotes Derby (England's oldest horse race, staged cross-country and first held in Yorkshire in 1519)

Fourth Sunday in Lent – Mothering Sunday (Originally a day off for domestic servants to return home to family and their 'mother' church)

1 – Meteorological spring starts/St David's
Day (Wales)

5 – National Day of Cornwall

12 – Farmers' Day (the name old tenant farmers gave
to St Gregory's Day, marked by sowing onions)

17 – St Patrick's Day (Ireland)

20 – County Durham Day

21 – Spring equinox

25 – Lady Day (quarter day when rents were due,
named after the Virgin Mary and nine months
before Christmas, this was an important rent day)

29 – West Riding of Yorkshire Day

April

Monday and Tuesday after Easter – Hocktide (a day
for raising parish funds and celebrated eagerly in
Hungerford, Berkshire)

1 – All Fools' Day

16 – Orkney Day

19 – Primrose Day (held in memory of British PM
Benjamin Disraeli whose favourite flower was
the primrose)

23 – St George's Day (England)

25 – Huntingdonshire Day

May

Seventh Sunday after Easter – Whitsun (an important Christian date which became the start of the 'Whitsuntide' holiday season)

Last Monday in May – Whitsun customs such as cheese-rolling and woolsack races

1 – May Day/Staffordshire Day

8 – Helston Flora Day (a world-famous Cornish festival marking the passing of winter)

9 – Liberation Day, Channel Islands (the national day of Jersey and Guernsey marking the end of Nazi occupation in 1945)

11 – Somerset Day

16 – County Day of Middlesex

29 – Oak Apple Day (see page 79)

June

First or second Sunday in June – Open Farm Sunday

1 – Meteorological summer starts/County Day of Dorset/Pembrokeshire Day

3 – World Cider Day

4 – County of Devon Day

5 – World Environment Day/Wiltshire Day

16 – Sussex Day

21 – Summer solstice/Shetland Flag Day/
Suffolk Day
24 – Midsummer Day (quarter day)

July

5 – Tynwald Day (the Isle of Man's National Day and
a public holiday)
15 – St Swithin's Day (see page 100)
23 – Historic County Flags Day (a colourful
celebration of the nation's centuries-old counties)
27 – County Day of Norfolk

August

A Saturday in August – National Plum Day (a
moveable event)
1 – Lammas/Yorkshire Day (originally 'loaf-mass',
celebrating the grain harvest with thanksgiving, fairs
and feasting)
5 – St Oswald's Day (County Day of Northumberland)
16 – St Roch's Day (once celebrated as the date of
Harvest Home and 'the great August festival of
the country')
22 – North Riding of Yorkshire Day
24 – East Riding of Yorkshire Day

September

First Saturday in September – Gloucester Day
Originally marked to celebrate the lifting of the
Siege of Gloucester in 1643
Middle Wednesday in September – UK Dairy Day
A Wednesday in September – Back British Farming
Day (a moveable event)
A high-profile awareness day for UK
food producers
1 – Meteorological autumn starts
13 – Rutland Day
23 – Autumn equinox
24 – County Day of Cumberland
25 – Monmouthshire Day
29 – Michaelmas (quarter day)/Westmorland Day

October

1 – County Day of Lincolnshire
19 – Oxfordshire Day
21 – Apple Day (dedicated to celebrating all things
apple, from pies and sauce to cider and juice)
26 – County Day of Essex
31 – All Hallows' Eve

November

Last Sunday before Advent – Stir-Up Sunday
(the day when families gather to prepare the
Christmas pudding)
Fourth Sunday before Christmas – Advent begins
1 – All Hallows' Day (All Saints' Day)
2 – All Souls' Day
5 – Bonfire Night
6 – St Illtud's Day (County Day of Glamorgan)
11 – Martinmas/Armistice Day (the feast day of St
Martin marked with merrymaking and preparations
for winter)
20 – St Edmund's Day (King of East Anglia and
original Patron Saint of England)
27 – Lancashire Day
28 – County Day of Caernarfonshire/
Bedfordshire Day
30 – St Andrew's Day (Scotland)

December

1 – Meteorological winter starts
21 – Winter solstice/St Thomas's Day
25 – Christmas Day (quarter day)
26 – St Stephen's Day/Boxing Day
31 – New Year's Eve

Further reading

There's a long and rich tradition of writing about nature, the countryside and rural life. You could even argue that it started with William the Conqueror's great survey of pastoral England, the Domesday Book, in 1086 (it didn't include major cities such as London, Winchester or Bristol). So the modern-day author has an endless number of potential sources, references and quotations. This selected bibliography lists the books which have been the most useful, reliable and inspiring in the creation of *Two for Joy* . . .

Baseley, Godfrey, *A Country Compendium* (Sidgwick & Jackson, 1977)

Brown, Jonathan, *Farming in the 1920s and '30s* (Shire Books, 2012)

Brown, Jonathan, *The Rural World of Eric Guy* (Old Pond Publishing, 2008)

Clapham, Veronica (editor), *Stow-on-the-Wold: Glimpses*

of the Past (Stow-on-the-Wold & District Civic Society, 2000)

Clifford, Sue and King, Angela, *The Apple Source Book* (Hodder & Stoughton, 2007)

Clifford, Sue and King, Angela, *Journeys Through England in Particular: On Foot* (Saltyard Books, 2014)

Coppin, Johnny (editor), *Forest and Vale and High Blue Hill* (Windrush Press, 1991)

Crawford, Peter (editor), *In the Country* (Macmillan, 1980)

Davis, Martin, *The Farmer and the Goose with the Golden Eyes* (Redcliffe Press, 2009)

Freeman, Eric, *Thumbsticks and Frails* (E. G. Freeman, 2010)

Garnett, Stephen (editor), *Traditional Counties of England* (DC Thomson, 2017)

Gascoigne, Bamber, *Encyclopaedia of Britain* (Macmillan, 1993)

Gibbings, L. V. (editor), *The Cotswold Sheep* (Geerings of Ashford, 1995)

Godwin, Fay and Toulson, Shirley, *The Drovers' Roads of Wales* (Wildwood House, 1978)

Grant, Russell, *The Real Counties of Britain* (Virgin Book, 1996)

Hamblyn, Richard, *The Met Office Cloud Book* (David & Charles, 2010)

Henson, Elizabeth, *British Sheep Breeds* (Shire Books, 1986)

Holden, Peter and Gregory, Prof Richard, *RSPB Handbook of British Birds* (Bloomsbury, 2021)

Humble, Kate and McGill, Martin, *Watching Waterbirds* (Bloomsbury, 2018)

Joad, C. E. M. (editor), *The English Counties Illustrated* (Odhams Press, 1949)

Lewis, June, *The Cotswolds: Life and Traditions* (Weidenfeld & Nicolson, 1996)

Martell, Charles, *Native Apples of Gloucestershire* (Hartpury Heritage Trust & Gloucestershire Orchard Trust, 2015)

Martell, Charles, *Native Plums (Prunus) of Gloucestershire* (Hartpury Heritage Trust & Gloucestershire Orchard Trust, 2018)

Martell, Charles, *Pears of Gloucestershire and Perry Pears of the Three Counties* (Hartpury Heritage Trust & Gloucestershire Orchard Trust, 2013)

Moule, Thomas, *The County Maps of Old England* (Studio Editions, 1990)

Palmer, Roy, *Britain's Living Folklore* (David & Charles, 1991)

Palmer, Roy, *Folklore of Gloucestershire* (Westcountry Books, 1994)

Phillips, Arthur (editor), *The BBC Book of the Countryside* (British Broadcasting Corporation, 1964)

Roud, Steve, *The English Year* (Penguin Books, 2006)

Russell, Tony, *The Illustrated Encyclopaedia of Trees of Britain and Europe* (Anness Publishing, 2017)

Scott-Macnab, Justine (editor), *Illustrated Encyclopaedia of Britain* (David & Charles, 1999)

Seymour, John, *The Forgotten Arts* (Dorling Kindersley, 1984)

Staelens, Yvette and Bearman, C. J., *Gloucestershire Folk Map* (Bournemouth University, 2010)

Staelens, Yvette and Bearman, C. J., *Hampshire Folk Map* (Bournemouth University, 2010)

Staelens, Yvette and Bearman, C. J., *Somerset Folk Map* (Bournemouth University, 2006)

Stout, Adam, *The Old Gloucester: The Story of a Cattle Breed* (Alan Sutton Publishing, 1980)

Various, *The British Heritage* (Odhams Press, 1948)

Various, *Sir Peter Scott at 80: A Retrospective* (Alan Sutton Publishing, 1989)

Varlow, Sally, *A Reader's Guide to Writers' Britain* (Prion Books, 1996)

Wainwright, Martin, *The English Village: History and Traditions* (Michael O'Mara Books, 2011)

Walkden, Paul, *The Wild Geese of the Newgrounds* (Friends of WWT Slimbridge, 2009)

Woolf, Jo, *Britain's Trees* (National Trust, 2020)

Wright, Geoffrey N., *The Cotswolds* (David & Charles, 1991)

Wright, John, *A Natural History of the Hedgerow* (Profile Books, 2017)

Wright, John, *A Spotter's Guide to Countryside Mysteries* (Profile Books, 2021)

Acknowledgements

Getting any book to print is a team effort and I've been incredibly fortunate to have a dedicated and experienced group of people around me from the outset. First, I must thank the professionals at Little, Brown who suggested the idea of this book to me, and especially Emily Barrett, Sarah Kennedy, Jon Appleton and Megan Phillips. Second, Gordon Wise at Curtis Brown who helped to get the project off the ground and offered his usual good judgement and insight.

Finding source material and checking facts was made easier by tapping into the wealth of knowledge, evidence and expertise that's found in the UK's wildlife, conservation and environmental organisations. I'm especially grateful to the British Trust for Ornithology (BTO), Buglife, the Bumblebee

Conservation Trust, Butterfly Conservation, the Campaign to Protect Rural England (CPRE), English Heritage, Linking Environment And Farming (LEAF), the Mammal Society, the Met Office, the National Farmers Union (NFU), the National Trust and the National Trust for Scotland, the People's Trust for Endangered Species, Plantlife, the Royal Horticultural Society, the Royal Society for the Protection of Birds (RSPB), the Wildlife Trusts and the Woodland Trust. Closer to home there were several organisations on my doorstep which proved to be invaluable; the Cotswold Voluntary Wardens, Cotswolds Conservation Board, Gloucestershire Geology Trust, Gloucestershire Naturalists' Society and the Wildfowl and Wetlands Trust at Slimbridge. Not forgetting the charity which protects and promotes the UK's endangered and native farm livestock, the Rare Breeds Survival Trust. It was created in 1973 with a certain Joe Henson as its founding chairman and to this day the Cotswold Farm Park proudly displays the handsome plaque awarded to Dad, which bears the charity's White Park cattle logo and the words: *Rare Breeds Survival Trust Approved Centre No.1.*

Many of the country sayings, farming tales and weather lore dotted through the book came courtesy of Eric Freeman. He has been a wonderful friend to the Henson family for more than fifty years and he's looked on like a favourite uncle by me and my sisters.

Not only is Eric generous in sharing his treasure trove of stories and anecdotes, he's also recorded them for posterity in print, audio and video. His excellent auto-biographical film, *Eric Freeman: A Legend in These Parts* is now on You Tube. Credit also goes to another great countryman and broadcaster, Brian Bailey, whose observations from a lifetime of watching wildlife, especially birds, were a superb resource. Hundreds of Brian's fascinating field recordings dating back more than thirty years are currently being preserved and curated by my collaborator on *Two for Joy*, Vernon Harwood. Sometimes it's no bad thing being a magpie! Other archives were also a rich vein of information and reminiscences, with the added bonus of being able to hear the authentic voices of important people, past and present. The collections held by British Pathé, the British Film Institute and the British Library all turned up gems, while the BBC Archive more than lived up to its first-rate reputation. Naturally enough editions of *Countryfile* and older TV programmes such as *Living Britain*, *In the Country* and several David Attenborough documentaries were a gift. The pick of network radio included episodes of *The Living World*, *Wildlife*, *The Countryside In* and *Sounds Natural*, and there was a wealth of material in three local radio programmes of the past; *Gloucestershire Country Matters*, *Lincolnshire Farming* and BBC Radio Oxford's *Countrywise*.

Elsewhere I was able to call upon the know-how of several organisations with excellent resources, collections or libraries: The Association of British Counties and its detailed gazetteer of 280,000 places; the Heritage Crafts Association with its red list of endangered crafts; the English Folk Dance and Song Society; Eynsham Morris and the recorded broadcasts of the village's most famous resident, historian and countrywoman, the late Mollie Harris (Martha Woodford in *The Archers*); and finally, the Museum of English Rural Life (MERL) in Reading which is a treasure house of documents, photographs and, most importantly, artefacts which tell the story of the countryside. Thank you, one and all.